I0202023

FOLLOW *the* WAY *of* LOVE

40 Devotional Stories for Caregivers

FOLLOW *the* WAY *of* LOVE

40 Devotional Stories for Caregivers

Cynthia A. Quattrocelli

Copyright © 2017 by Cynthia Quattrocelli

All rights reserved. This book or any part thereof
may not be reproduced or used in any manner whatsoever
without the express written permission of the publisher
except for the use of brief quotations in a book review.

Printed in the United States of America
First Printing, 2017
ISBN 0692921605

4900 LaCross Road
North Charleston, SC 29406
http://www.apub.com

Photos usage rights: all photos in this book are "labeled for reuse/public domain."

Unless otherwise noted, Scriptures are taken from the Holy Bible, New International Version Copyright © 1973, 1978, 1984 by International Bible Society. Used by permission of International Bible Society.

"NIV" and "New International Version" are trademarks registered in the United States Patent and Trademark office by International Bible Society.

Scripture quotations marked The Message Bible are taken from THE MESSAGE: The New Testament, Psalms, and Proverbs by Eugen H. Peterson. Copyright © 1993, 1994, 1995. Used by permission of NavPress Publishing

Scripture quotations marked The Amplified® Bible (AMPC), are taken from The Holy Bible, Amplified Version by Zondervan Copyright © 1954, 1958, 1962, 1964, 1965, 1987 by The Lockman Foundation. Used by permission. (www.Lockman.org)

With

utmost

honor,

I dedicate

this book to

Almighty God

for His

loving care ...

seen daily.

God's Living Word

continues to guide me

as I follow the way of love,

while serving those in need.

He is

the Ultimate

Caregiver!

CONTENTS

CONTENTS

CONTENTS

Acknowledgments:

I thank the Lord for my husband's guidance and help at connecting meaningful messages to several of these devotional stories. Also, Jim is the one who gave me the idea of adding pages of photos with corresponding scriptural verses.

Acknowledgment and thanks goes to two other caregivers who contributed their stories of God's intervention as they fulfilled daily assignments. Catherine Chambers and Arlene Quadnow wrote touching accounts of how they saw God using them to bless hurting people.

Cathy is my twin sister. She has served as a Spiritual Care Leader and Activities Leader in nursing homes and Assisted Living facilities. Arlene is a dear friend. Her experience includes working as a P.C.A. (Personal Care Aide) in Assisted Living facilities and presently is an in-home care provider.

Thanks goes to my friend Patti Reffo who kindly offered to help me with the grammatical and structural necessities for this book. She is a retired teacher with a heart full of God's love.

Recognition and appreciation to *The Alzheimer's Association* and to *Cross Country Education* for the training that I have received which in turn has increased my achievements in therapeutic approaches to dementia.

INTRODUCTION

Introduction:

Can you find a title below that describes you as a caregiver?

- Activity Leader
- Chaplain
- Children's Day-Care Teacher
- Companion Aide
- Counselor
- Dementia Care Provider
- Doctor
- Emergency Medical Technician
- Friend
- Foster Care Provider
- Grandparent
- Hospice Care Provider
- Missionary
- Nanny
- Neighbor
- Nurse
- Nursing Assistant
- Parent
- Pastor
- Personal Care Aide
- School Bus Driver
- Sibling
- Social Worker
- Spouse
- Teacher
- Therapist
- Volunteer

Each of the assignment names listed above has at its foundation taking care of the needs of another. Whether it be caring for an elderly person, a child, your own family, or for those with an acute or a chronic illness, the role of caregiver is close to the heart of God. Caregiver describes a person who gives direct care. There are other names we associate with the practice of Caregiving not mentioned here in this book. Whatever your title may be, you are an exceptional person that has made a profound difference in the world.

Alzheimer's disease has become more prevalent in our communities for the last few decades. *Follow the Way of Love* includes narratives revealing God's intervention during some typical situations that myself and two other caregivers experienced while overseeing ill patients, elderly people, and those with Alzheimer's disease. Included in this book, are stories testifying of God's help when the care was for children. With influence from the Holy Spirit and the evidence of God's loving Presence I have witnessed treasured moments unfold during some very trying circumstances. Please note: we have given fictitious names to those whom we have written about to protect their identities.

My main goal in offering these examples of God's leading during care is to honor Him and to encourage caregivers toward a stronger bond with the Lord. In the index section, find 135 Bible verses specifically related to caregiving. Applying God's Word will provide you with support and direction for every situation you experience while carrying out this role. Attending to others is a challenging task, but with God's loving Strength, you will see good come from your input.

I have written this book as an instructional tool to show others what has helped me in giving His loving care to the hurting. I am passing on my own testimonies of enjoyed adventures in the field of care-giving with a hope for caregivers to advance toward a more intimate walk with God. The reader is welcome to discover that our God is alive, active, and approachable, every day!

The stories here derive from real experiences of serving the Lord as Activities Assistants, Dementia Care Program Leaders, In-Home Companion Aides, Nannies, Neighbors, Nurses, Nursing Assistants, Personal Care Aides, Spiritual Care Leaders, and Volunteers.

Throughout the book, you will find pages with the following heading: *Activity Ideas for People with Dementia.* Each of these pages list successful approaches that I have found valuable for increasing the quality of life for those with dementia. I share practical methods and activities I have learned or developed myself to help people who have short-term memory impairment / dementia. These activities have been known to help people with dementia keep certain life-learned skills. In addition, I have randomly placed pages with *Bible verses with snapshots.* Enjoy reading the scripture verse corresponding with the theme of the photo.

Bible scriptures help us to see the devoted and caring nature of our Heavenly Father. Therefore, each true narrative in this book offers two scripture verses to emphasize the message in the devotional story. A prayer coming from a caregiver's viewpoint and verses for meditation complete each story. All scripture is from the New International Version, unless specified as from the Amplified version, or from The Message Bible.

Find a special place to meet alone with God daily. Enter His Presence with thanksgiving and praise. I find that many believers express how they do not have time to be alone with God. I see it this way, we cannot afford not to go to Him daily. Especially when it comes to the overwhelming responsibility of attending to fragile and sick people, we need wisdom and favor from above.

Open your mouth and talk with God candidly. Thankfulness honors God (Psalm 50:23). Recognize all the blessings in your life. This is always a good place to start. He longs to be with you and His desire is to father you. Petition Father God for your needs by declaring His promises from the written Word. I always say, "Don't despair—instead declare!" Proclaim His Word. I believe this honors Him. Christ is the Living Word. He is an ever-present help in trouble. Delight yourself in the Lord; He cares very much for you.

Do you know Jesus as your Savior?

Our Lord Jesus followed through with God's original Care Plan for the redemption of all humankind, by willingly going to the cross; He is the only acceptable sacrifice for our sins. Jesus said, "I am the Way, the Truth, and the Life. No one comes to the Father, except through Me" (John 14:6).

Everyone by faith, who calls on the Name of the Jesus, confessing and repenting from their sins will be saved (Romans 10:13). We can have eternal life because it is a free-gift from God and not by works so that no man can boast (Ephesians 2:8-9). Make a declaration of your new faith to another. Jesus now lives in your heart; you have the confirmation of life eternal with God.

You are now born-again if you believe in your heart that Christ died for your sins. You have the promised Holy Spirit, but pray too for a greater infilling of the Holy Spirit (the baptism in the Holy Spirit). Read about the manifestation and the gifts of the Holy Spirit in 1 Corinthians 12-14. God has good plans for you (Jeremiah 29:11). Ask the Lord to show you His will for your life and gifts and talents He designed in you.

Follow the Way of Love and use your specific spiritual gifts and talents when helping people. The power of prayer is so available and essential to help Christian caregivers. In addition, you can be a Light to those you are attending to by purposefully treating them in accordance to God's Word. I have heard it said, that the lifestyle we as Christians live out in our daily lives by following the example of Christ may be the only Bible some people will ever read. People should see Christ in you whenever you are near them.

Praying for the people you come across while being a care provider can build your faith too, especially when you see God move on their behalf. Pray for the Holy Spirit to draw them close to the Lord and keep on planting seeds of the gospel. Leave the ones you care for with a fragrant trace of Christ's love. Caregivers, you ought to see people feeling better because God's Goodness in you just visited them today. We are Ambassadors for Christ. Through our testimonies of His Goodness, many will gain faith to put their hope in Jesus Christ. Amen.

The Best News – Cynthia Quattrocelli

Lord, when did we see you hungry and feed you, or thirsty and give you something to drink? When did we see you a stranger and invite you in or needing clothes and clothe you? When did we see you sick or in prison and go to visit you? The King will reply, "I tell you the truth, whatever you did for one of the least of these brothers of mine, you did for me." - Matthew 25:37-40

"For God so loved the world that He gave His one and only Son, that whoever believes in Him shall not perish, but have eternal life. For God, did not send His Son into the world to condemn the world, but to save the world through Him. Whoever believes in Him is not condemned, but whoever does not believe stands condemned already because he has not believed in the name of God's one and only Son. - John 3:16-18

The form of the man under the covers with face unseen appeared emaciated from a chronic disease. Just the day before, I saw police escorting ill prisoners from a nearby penitentiary throughout the first floor of the hospital. Some of those guarded wore orange-striped clothing and dragged chains around their ankles; others in this group were on stretchers. I quickly realized as I entered this patient's room, he was one of those from the prison brought in for medical care. He may have been in the last stages of the HIV/AIDS Virus; not sure.

My job working as an Activity Leader in this county hospital was to visit while offering some type of sensory, social, or cognitive stimulation for every patient on my list.

Sizing up the situation, the Lord showed me this man did not have long to live. How then could I offer recreational therapy? Certainly, it would not be offering to throw a ball, play catch, listen to a tune, or to look at baseball cards.

Sitting in a chair near the bed, I greeted him and introduced myself. I had a burden for his soul. I began to give him the Gospel message reciting John 3:16. When I finished, I asked this question: "Sir, would you like to receive Christ as your Savior - being sure you will go to Heaven when you die?" With his face still under the covers, the man nodded. Watching the bed sheet move, I thought, "This was a genuine acceptance of faith in Christ." My heart flooded with joy. I felt hopeful he believed in the One who offered *the best news* at this hour of his life. He did not say a word in our short visit together, nevertheless I sensed an eternal optimism from his quick response.

The next day at the morning report staff meeting, I learned the man had expired during the night. With tears, I thanked God for using me to bring the hope of glory to this man. Someday, I will meet this redeemed man face-to-face in Heaven where nothing will cover up the Light on his face. Praise the Lord!

Prayer: Father God, use me today as an Ambassador for the Kingdom of God. As a caregiver, I want to be the vessel or instrument You have prepared to carry Your Word of hope to the people in my path. My prayer is that the destiny of those You have put in my care become redirected when given a chance to repent. I pray that once saved, they will make Jesus Christ the Lord of their life. I believe the Holy Spirit is guiding me on how to share Christ as the Way, the Truth, and the Life, even with those who may appear to be unreachable. Lord, I know the Holy Spirit goes before me softening and making ready their hearts for the Gospel. I want to lovingly follow through and obey His leading. In Jesus' Name. Amen.

Meditate on: Matthew 28:18-20, Luke 15:7, John 14:1-6,

Hebrews 13:3

Flower Girls – by Cynthia Quattrocelli

My frame was not hidden from You when I was made in the secret place. When I was woven together in the depths of the earth, Your eyes saw my unformed body. All the days ordained for me were written in Your Book before one of them came to be. -Psalm 139:15-16

"For I know the plans I have for you, "declares the Lord, "plans to prosper you and not to harm you, plans to give you hope and a future." -Jeremiah 29:11

Grandma was dear to me and to my identical twin sister, Cathy. We were special in her heart, too. With delight, she would proudly introduce us as her "twin granddaughters"! In our early thirties, we were still single women. Our plan was to sell our beauty salon and move to Florida.

In the last few months of preparation before we drove over the rainbow to the warmth of the Sunshine State, we both noted a distinct inner witness of something wonderful coming in our lives. We felt drawn to watch church services on TV; this was a new interest for us because we had not been to church since we were seven years old.

In addition, soon after our move to Florida was complete, we both shared an identical leading to buy flowers to pass out to the elderly at a local nursing home.

24

This was profound because we both had the same idea on the same day. We were not yet Born-Again. I was saved a year later. It then became clear; the Holy Spirit had been drawing us to Christ and had anointed us for ministry to the elderly.

God put such a love in our hearts for older people, especially those who are ill. Years later, after working for some time in nursing homes as an Activities Leader, this anointing was confirmed to me when the Lord spoke in my spirit, "Your job has been a calling on your life."

Yes, God sets up our beginnings as stated in Psalm 139:16, "All the days ordained for me were written in Your Book before one of them came to be." I am sure Grandma was praying for us while we prepared to move South. I do not doubt her quiet faith and private prayers are what God heard and His Holy Spirit drew us to the Lord Jesus. It has been 34 years since I invited this Wonderful Someone, my Lord and Savior Jesus Christ to come and live in my heart.

Through the years, both Cathy and I have sought out God's direction when caring for the elderly. While working in nursing homes, my sister and I quite possibly have been considered as, the *flower girls* by the residents when passing out floral arrangements. This has continued to be one of the activities we have used for sensory stimulation and socialization. God even had that small act of kindness planned, because He knows all the plans He has for us.

You may be in the trial of choosing a life career; put your trust in Him. He does know all about you and wants to share with you the plans of good He designed just for you. Ask Him to open right doors and close wrong doors for employment. Psalm 37:23 in the Amplified Bible says; The steps of a (good and righteous) man/woman are directed and established by the Lord, and He delights in his way (and blesses his path).

Prayer: Dear Father God, I am Your servant. I delight in You. The plans You have prepared for me are by far the best. Help me to rest and to wait with faith and patience as You develop and guide me toward that destiny. I believe You have shown to me clues throughout my life as to what specifically I am called to do. I know that in all things You work for the good to those who love You, and who have been called according to Your purpose (Romans 8:28). Help me to recognize the path I am to be on for Your glory. In Jesus name, Amen.

Meditate on: Psalm 32:8, Psalm 139, Jeremiah 29:11-13,

Ephesians 2:10

"God has not Forgotten You!"- by Catherine Chambers

Before a word is on my tongue, You know it completely, O Lord. -Psalm 139:4

Casting all your anxiety on Him, for He cares for you. -1Peter 5:7

Serving now as a Spiritual Care Leader, I recall back to my very first day visiting as a volunteer in this skilled nursing facility. Entering the activity room, I noticed a small group of residents scattered around the room and all were facing the television. Nervously, I walked over to a woman curled up in a geriatric chair. Sadly, I saw how her body was not able to stretch out. Her back was in an extremely hunched over position. It seemed impossible for her to relax her backbone.

I said, "hello, my name is Cathy." She told me her name. Then I said to her, "God has not forgotten you!" It was difficult for her to tilt or to turn her head towards me, so I knelt. Our eyes met. As soon as she heard my words, she began to cry uncontrollably.

Minutes passed by before she stopped crying and could speak to me. She thanked me. I believe the words I had told her were straight from our compassionate Father God and given to her for comfort. She began to have a joyful demeanor unlike before. Truly, we were both touched by the Lord's care and loving-kindness that day.

Two weeks later, this special lady passed on to eternity in the arms of our Loving Savior.

Recently, I had a sermon prepared to preach to those who had gathered in the dining room for Church. Those present came either in a wheelchair, a Geri-chair, led by the arm of a caretaker/family member or walked in using an assistive-device. I addressed the heaviness apparent in their hearts from what many had made known to me through the week.

Most had been suffering from depression because of being lonely and forgotten, as they described it. They shared how family did not come to visit often enough or not at all. Some were grieving their loss of independence and others were in pain. I told them to be honest with God and cry out to Him, to lay it all out to Him, and to call upon the name of the Lord Jesus. My scripture verse was, God knows your thoughts from afar, cast all your concerns upon Him for He really does care for you and has not forgotten any of you (1 Peter 5:7).

Psalm 145:9 exclaims, the Lord is good to all; He has compassion on all He has made. Revelation 21:4 promises hope for those who are in faith; He will wipe away every tear and there is no pain or illness in Heaven. These are loving Words from our Lord for each one, whether we are the cared-for or the caregiver.

As care providers, we too can become frustrated, feel alone, and become tired out from doing so much for the person we have charge over. Let Christ be your Peace. God tells us in Jeremiah 29:13, "You will seek Me and find Me when you seek Me with all your heart." Family members share with me about the loss they feel because of their loved one's physical or cognitive decline. My hope and prayer for them is to remember that God heals the brokenhearted (Psalm 147:3). He hears the cry of the righteous. We can get through each day as we wait upon the Lord and trust Him for the next phase of life. Believe His word by speaking it over situations! Then go about each day declaring what you hope for. God honors faith.

Caregivers, thank Him for the opportunity to help people - doing unto them what you would have them do unto you. Imagine yourself in their shoes to gain understanding of what they are going through. Look for opportunities to do what you can to encourage them. When you help another; you are helped! Count your blessings every morning. Spend time in worship. Come close to Him and He will come close to you - You will notice God's Strength and Goodness often through the day, if you anticipate it. He does give rest to the weary.

Prayer: I praise You Lord and thank You for using me to bless others with Words of hope. May I never doubt how Faithful You are to keep Your Promises. You will forever love me and those who need my care. You are so close to all who call on You. Thank You King of Kings for never leaving us nor forsaking us. I am glad to know the God of all comfort. I praise You with thanksgiving in my heart and I am strengthened by your caring Presence. May I continue receiving from You reassuring words to say to the elderly, the sick, and the bed-bound. It is a joy to serve You, Lord of All. Amen.

Meditate on: Psalm 4:1, Psalm 145, Isaiah 41:10, Matthew 6:25-34, 2 Corinthians 5:1-21

Hope in Any Language - by Arlene Quadnow

You are all sons of God through faith in Christ Jesus, for all of you who were baptized into Christ have clothed yourselves with Christ. There is neither Jew nor Greek, slave nor free, male nor female, for you are all one in Christ Jesus. -Galatians 3:26-28

For to me, to live is Christ and to die is gain. -Philippians 1:21

As a Personal Care Aide, I help people who come from many cultures. One day, I was getting "Mama Rita" ready for her bath. She was born in India, and she speaks about five words in English. With a very conversational tone, she looked at me and spoke in her language. Her husband interpreted. She said, "When I die, I am going to Heaven to be with God and when you die, you will be in Heaven with God and me." Mama Rita has Alzheimer's disease, so this brightened the moment of a rather weary and mundane task ahead.

In Matthew 5, Jesus teaches the Beatitudes to the crowds. The Message Bible for verse 7 reads like this; "You're blessed when you care. At the moment, of being care-full, you find yourselves being cared for". Mama Rita may have noted my job was one requiring care and mercy and it prompted her to say what she did. It was beautiful to hear in her own words the certainty of her faith and her hope of going to live in Heaven with God someday. Faith is *hope in any language.*

Prayer: Heavenly Father, thank You for those moments when blessings and encouragement come through the person I am caring for by their words or deeds. Help me to take the opportunity to bless them too in some way while they are in my care. For what good is it if a man claims to have faith but has no deeds? I ask You Father God for wisdom as I give helpful attentiveness to others. In Jesus, Amen.

Meditate on: Proverbs 9:10-12, Philippians 4:4-14, James 1, John 3:16-18

The Sunshine Club – by Cynthia Quattrocelli

Let us not become weary in doing good, for at the proper time we will reap a harvest if we do not give up. Therefore, as we have opportunity let us do good to all people, especially to those who belong to the family of believers. -Galatians 6:9-10

In the same way, let your light shine before men, that they may see your good deeds and praise your Father in heaven. -Matthew 5:16

Helen was a sweet lady who resided at an assisted living home where I was hired to organize and lead the Dementia Group Activities Program. This resident had been diagnosed with dementia and was considered non-verbal. Nursing staff routinely placed her in the lobby sitting in a wheelchair. Most days I saw her asleep, and she was difficult to awaken.

One day as I went about the task of rounding up residents who were in our *Sunshine Club,* I stopped and sat on the bench near her. After calling her name and touching her hand, she awoke and looked straight in my eyes. As with all the other mornings since I had started this group nine months earlier, I invited her to come to our activities gathering. This time, without thinking I would get an answer, I asked her if she knew my name. Helen smiled and with a sweet Southern accent simply said, "Why yes, your name is Cindy, and you're a pretty little thing."

This answer delighted me because of the following: The daily routine of reintroducing myself again to her, along with her consistent participation in the group activities, was making an impact on her as evidenced by her remembering and verbalizing my name. I also was surprised when she inserted the additional comment.

After months of daily participation in the program, she had become familiar with my presence. Eventually with encouragement, she enthusiastically reminisced when given a subject from her era, sang old hymns off a song sheet, and even initiated an offer to recite poems she recalled from childhood.

Nursing staff would drop by occasionally as *the Sunshine Club* was in progress and marvel at the difference they saw in the residents while engaged in a meaningful activity. They would often comment how they had not realized certain residents still had the ability to verbalize. They saw positive change in the same people they had been told had no possibility of participating.

Of course, the best involvement is of the Spiritual kind. It is very sweet to watch Senior Saints joining in with the sing-a-longs. Most can read from the hymn sheets, some can recall the words, others are attentive, and you may even see their feet tapping to the tune. At any age, it is lovely to dwell in the Presence of the Lord. Worshiping Him leads us to His dwelling place (Psalm 84:1).

When this happens, God's peace is present for restoring hope. Indeed, a Son-Shine Club can develop each time we meet and focus on Him. God bless the elderly; I refer to them as diamonds and jewels.

Prayer: Heavenly Father, thank You for giving me the opportunity to care for the Senior population. I like to describe them as diamonds and jewels. If we look close, we can still see their unique personality sparkle from within. In the Bible, it says to honor your Mother and Father and it will go well with you. Because I am created in Your image and strive for the likeness of Christ, I aim to do unto others as I would want them to do unto me. When I am older, I believe I will have kind people to help me, too. But for right now, as one who attends to the necessities of others, I will give the best care I can. Your Word says my giving will be given back to me in the same measure I give. In Jesus Name, Amen.

Meditate on: Psalm 37:5-6, Psalm 92:12-15, Psalm 108:1-3, Hebrews 6:10

Activity Ideas for People with Dementia

Activity Participation:

In my years of helping people with dementia, I recorded their response to a steady schedule of cognitive, sensory, social, physical, and spiritual activities. The results included fulfilled goals aimed at maintaining life-learned skills.

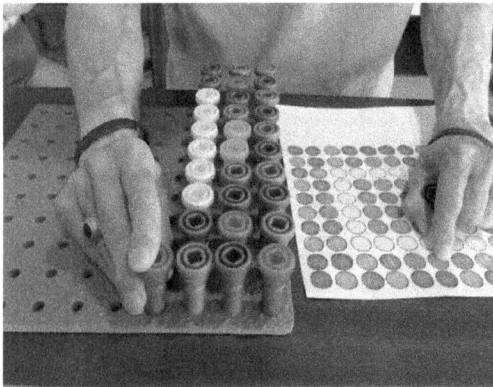

I believe creative and structured programs combined with a gentle reassurance can produce optimal levels of participation from individuals with Dementia.

The completion of activities for people with dementia can produce a higher self-confidence resulting in an improved quality of life.

I have seen an increase in verbalization, less agitation, decreased levels of combativeness and less fall injuries when residents were engaged in age-appropriate activities designed for individuals with dementia. These results were particularly apparent during the typical sun-downing time period (behavior changes in persons with dementia during late afternoon hours).

Even the Very Hairs of Your Head Are All Numbered
- by Arlene Quadnow

In everything I did, I showed you that by this kind of hard work we must help the weak, remembering the words the Lord Jesus Himself said; "It is more blessed to give than to receive". - Acts 20:35

Do not let any unwholesome talk come out of your mouths, but only what is helpful for building others up in accordance to their needs, that it may benefit those who listen. - Ephesians 4:29

Toward the end of my shift and after a particularly long day at the assisted living facility where I worked as a Personal Care Aide, I attended to "Rosie." When I completed making her bed, she looked at me and said, "Has anyone ever told you that you have beautiful hair?" I turned toward her and smiled. "Why, thank you," I said. Her blue eyes glistened with life.

I realized little gems like this are what make all I do worthwhile. Her words reminded me of Christ's teaching; *even the very hairs of your head are all numbered.* Not one of us is forgotten by God. He loves you and me!

Prayer: Father, I am glad for little, but joyful moments in life when another person will touch our hearts with words of affirmation - they lift us up. Thank You for knowing my coming and going. You keep an eye on me every day. I am the apple-of-Your-eye. Help me to keep in step with the Holy Spirit for producing the fruit of love, joy, peace, patience, kindness, goodness, faithfulness, gentleness, and self-control while helping the sick and the poor. In Jesus' Name, Amen.

Meditate on: Psalm 17:8, Proverbs 31:26, Luke 12:7, Galatians 5:22, Ephesians 5:1

A Time to Dance - by Arlene Quadnow

There is a time to mourn and a time to dance. -Ecclesiastes 3:4

Do nothing out of selfish ambition or vain conceit, but in humility consider others better than yourselves. Each of you should look not only to your own interests, but to the interests of others. -Philippians 2:3-4

Many times, there was entertainment at the assisted living facility where I worked as a Nursing Assistant. Sally, who lived in the Memory Care unit, loved music and enjoyed dancing to it. One day, I happened to have a break during the entertainment program. Sally was inviting many people from fellow residents to staff members for *a time to dance.* No one came forth. I knew it was time I stepped out to join her.

We danced with such abandonment and freedom. For a moment in time, she was not the confused elderly woman with dementia. I saw a young lady dancing her heart out with such joy. Sally, in her childlike way, had taught me to enjoy the present. There is a season for every activity under Heaven. There is a time to mourn and a *time to dance.*

A consistent intake of God's Word provides guidance for every season of life. On my own, I am not good at memorizing information. This includes remembering scripture. But, I have come to realize, if I take time daily to nourish myself in God's Word, I am in step with the Holy Spirit. He then downloads scriptures for applying to good times and to challenging times in life.

Prayer: Dear Heavenly Father, I am so blessed because I hear the Holy Spirit directing me through the Word of God hidden in my heart. He reminds me to be kind to others. Thank You for reminding me to consider other people's interests above my own as I assist ill family members, elderly residents, patients, or whomever I am helping. My desire is to recognize the timing of the Holy Spirit, to live in harmony with others, and be sympathetic to all. In Jesus' Name, Amen.

Meditate on: Psalm 30:11, Psalm 118:24, 1 Thessalonians 5:14-16,

1 Peter 5:5

A Divine Appointment – by Cynthia Quattrocelli

Now we know that if the earthly tent we live in is destroyed, we have a building from God, an eternal house in Heaven, not built by human hands. -2 Corinthians 5:1

Jesus answered him, "I tell you the truth, today you will be with me in paradise". -Luke 23:43

It turned out to be a worthwhile task when earlier I took the extra effort to pull from storage some old Gospel records. Strategically, I arranged the old record player in the lounge room at the county hospital nursing home. My plan was to play music for the group of elderly residents gathered there. As an Activity Leader, one of my goals was to get the folks involved in sing-a-longs. The recognizable hymns provided both Spiritual and cognitive input to encourage a verbal response.

At first, the drowsy residents in the room didn't even notice I had turned off the television. Now with the music coming forth, suddenly there was a Sweet Spirit in the room. A few faces glowed as they sang along to the familiar words. Some closed their eyes, but others were following my lead as I cheered them on to join in. At one point, I was singing loudly with a person who seemed to be getting joy out of crooning to the old Spiritual song, "Swing Low, Sweet Chariot."

After we all had a grand time singing together, I was thinking - this morning's program had gone very well. I had offered sensory, cognitive, social, and spiritual stimulation which produced a noted response. The residents at this long-term care facility would have had no other prompting that day other than having staff help with their dressing, feeding, and bathing.

Moments later, I was pulling my Activity cart loaded down with music equipment and other paraphernalia through the unit, when three Nursing Assistants motioned me to come into a certain resident's room.

Excitedly, they told me how they heard through the wall of this resident's room, the "Swing Low, Sweet Chariot" song I had just sung with the other folks. Then with much emotion, they explained how they felt the song had ushered their beloved resident into Heaven while she was taking her last few breaths.

You see, the head of her bed was directly up against the wall of the lounge room where I had held the sing-a-long. She was a believer in Christ. We were all inspired by faith that although her earthly tent no longer was active, she was now living in her new home prepared by our Savior. The staff were notably overwhelmed. The "band of angels" ushered her into paradise just as the song announces and they had the chance to say their good-byes.

I was blessed to see how the Goodness of the Lord had touched the hearts of the workers as God displayed His Sweet Presence during her parting. It was *a Divine appointment.*

Prayer: Father God, my prayer is to follow the way of love and eagerly use the Spiritual Gifts You provide me. I am available each day to serve You wherever my feet take me. Help me to be ready in season and out of season to present the Gospel of God's Grace to everyone (2 Timothy 4:2). Thank You for Your Son's sacrifice for our sins. I have this Good News to proclaim to all who are in my path. I yield to You, Almighty God - I give my future days to You - waiting for Divine appointments to bring the Hope of Glory to the lost. In Jesus' Name, Amen.

Meditate on: John 11:25, 2 Corinthians 15:51-54,

Philippians 3:20-21, Hebrews 1:14

Activity Ideas for People with Dementia
Sensory Stimulation Techniques:

For people displaying unresponsiveness or a low-functioning ability level, I have prompted them by using sensory stimulation. This has served to maintain their eye-contact and at times triggered an attempt at verbalization.

Activities can be designed to incorporate the five senses: visual, auditory, tactile (the sense of touch), gustatory (the sense of taste), and olfactory (the sense of smell).

Pet therapy is a fun way to provide sensory stimulation leading to reminiscing and communication.

I have provided sensory stimulation techniques in conjunction with socialization to non-verbal residents. It can bring about a manifestation of evident-alertness or facial grimaces. With a person who displays little interaction to stimuli from their daily environment, this can be significant.

This type of response may not seem as a monumental achievement to most, but for the person with limited communication abilities, it can be a proof to them that they are still connecting with others, thus giving them a better quality of life. This exchange usually brings some comfort to their family.

Honoring Others Above Myself – by Cynthia Quattrocelli

Praise be to the God and Father of our Lord Jesus Christ, the Father of compassion and the God of all comfort, who comforts us in all our troubles, so that we can comfort those in any trouble with the comfort we ourselves have received from God. -2 Corinthians 1:3-4

If anyone has material possessions and sees his brother in need, but has no pity on him, how can the love of God be in him? -1 John 3:17

I remember feeling so fearful in my very first recreation therapy job. I had obtained an A.A.S. degree in the Occupational Therapy Assistant Program after going back to school at age 39. Because I liked arts and crafts, I chose to use this degree to work in recreation therapy with residents who lived in nursing homes.

This county hospital, long-term care unit was my first nursing home setting. It was (what I thought at the time) a very scary environment. Although I knew God had called me and prepared me for the assignment, fear set in and I had a sense of being in the wrong job. Everywhere I looked, people were suffering in ways that appeared too hopeless. I did not know how to talk to them, nevertheless how to help them. Patients there were not who I had pictured myself caring for. What I expected was the sweet old grandpas and grandmas living in a nursing home and who would be pleased to have me come and help them with recreational activities aimed at keeping their physical and social skills, etc.

Instead, at this first experience, there were residents in every age bracket diagnosed with things like multiple sclerosis, dementia due to excessive illegal drug use, comatose victims from car and motorcycle wrecks, obesity due to diabetes therefore bed-ridden, aged Down Syndrome folks, people with the HIV virus, etc. Only a small percentage living there were elderly who suffered from ailments primarily familiar to the older population such as a status post CVA/stroke.

Eventually, looking not at the afflictions of the majority there and how I had no prior experience working with these types of physical and cognitive complications, I became determined to be productive in the best way I could. A brief time passed; I had learned all the names of the 120 residents because I made it a point to provide them with a room visit, weekly. Discovering what I could about each of their leisure time interests from the past and up to that present time helped me provide them with quality recreational activities.

Recalling God's Word in the book of James, the 2nd chapter, where it is explaining to love your neighbor as yourself and not show favoritism, I allowed my heart to be redirected by obedience. James teaches that God is no respecter of persons. I should not have been fearful or had negative thoughts toward these residents because of what their ailments showed outwardly. They needed a friend. After only a few months of helping them, I began to see that this job was a blessing indeed.

As time went on, it got easier to look past the outer afflictions to see the soul of the person within. I made many friends with the residents. To some, I became like family. This first job in a hospital, set me up for the love I now have at working in such settings to help people cope and find hope in God.

There is no greater reward than to be used by the Lord to aid another in their suffering even in a small way. Christ said, "When you give a banquet, invite the poor, the crippled, the lame, the blind, and you will be blessed" (Luke 14:13). I am no longer uneasy around someone I meet for the first time just because they look, talk, walk, or have evidence of a cognitive decline. In our world, there is a banquet-full of souls that come with a variety of hardships; all need encouragement. I am grateful that the Lord used this experience to develop in me a quest for *honoring others above myself.*

Pray and allow the meekness and gentleness of the Lord to lead you to where He can use you to build up those who are low. Look for the evidence of His Hand moving on your behalf. Anticipate an answer. If you think you are not in the right place, then pray that He will help you to see how it may turn into the RIGHT place, for Him to work through you. You can also pray that He will open Right doors that no man can shut.

Prayer: Come let us sing for joy to the Lord, the Maker of Heaven and earth. Father God, You are good to all; You have compassion on all You have made. May all people know of Your mighty acts by what Your saints speak to them about. Lord, guide me and teach me in the ways I should go and establish the works of my hands for me as You have promised to do. Help me to stay seeking the Living Word upon which I develop maturity having all that I need; I will abound in every good work. Thank You for the blessing of caring for others; My capability comes from You. Father God, continue to make me competent as a minister of the new covenant. In Jesus Name, Amen.

Meditate on: Isaiah 53:1-12, Isaiah 58:6-14, 2 Corinthians 1:4-11,

1 Timothy 5:16

"I Do!" – by Cynthia Quattrocelli

Train up a child in way he should go, and when he is old, he will not turn from it. -Proverbs 22:6

Therefore, anyone who humbles himself like this little child is greater in the kingdom of Heaven. -Matthew 18:4

Mandy surprised and delighted me one day when she enthusiastically declared, *"I do"* from the back seat of the car. This was a response of faith from the youngster I was taking care of. As her Nanny since she was ten months old and now age five, we spent a lot of time in the car driving around town doing errands for the whole family.

For our outing that day, I brought with me a children's CD for her to listen to as we drove from place to place fulfilling each mission. When I pulled into the parking lot of the plaza, Mandy un-buckled her seatbelt in haste.

She had been sitting in the back listening intently to the person on the CD sharing Bible stories. Between each story, a chorus of children sang catchy songs about God's love. They emphasized the message about having faith in Jesus. When the commentator asked the audience if there was anyone out there that would like to receive Jesus as their Savior, Mandy jumped forward grabbing the back of the seat next to me. In joyful enthusiasm, she made her declaration of faith in Christ. What a thrill for me to be the one God used to direct this child to find Christ.

It was not long before this 5-year-old was letting her Light shine before most of the people in her life. When I took her to get her hair cut, she boldly proclaimed the whole Gospel to the barber who was cutting her hair. She proclaimed her faith in a loud voice. This was her usual custom of speaking; she shouted out every sentence. There was not a person in the shop that day who did not hear the gospel message. She was ecstatic at discovering Jesus' love.

As a caregiver, find creative ideas to guide people of all ages to the Goodness of God. Everyday assignments can provide opportunities toward witnessing while using our God given gifts. Even though I do not sing or narrate stories on CD, I used other people's gifts to have Mandy hear about God's love and then have a chance to declare Jesus as her Savior. They say, the best gift is the one needed at the time. You never know who is watching and listening. You may be the one blessed to see another's life changed for eternity. There is nothing better. What gift can you use?

In the book of Romans chapter 10, Apostle Paul teaches that Christ is the end of the law. With the New Covenant through Christ's sacrifice on the cross, righteousness is by faith. It says: The Word is near you; it is in your mouth and in your heart. If you confess with your mouth, "Jesus is Lord," and believe in your heart that God raised Him from the dead, you will be saved. Share the Message.

Prayer: Heavenly Father, thank you for the best opportunities and creative ideas available to me at the right time to witness the great love of Christ Jesus. You are able to do immeasurably more than all I ask or imagine, according to Your Power that is at work within me (Ephesians 3:20). I believe You have gone before me breaking up hardened hearts and preparing souls for the Gospel of Love. I hope and pray they will call upon You - coming in humility just like a child. In Jesus Name, Amen.

Meditate on: Matthew 18:10-14, Acts 2:38-39, Acts 16:31-34, Revelation 3:20

Jesus Saves – by Cynthia Quattrocelli

Therefore, encourage one another and build each other up, just as in fact you are doing. – 1 Thessalonians 5:11

Finally, all of you, live in harmony with one another; be sympathetic, love as brothers, be compassionate and humble. - 1 Peter 3:8

Just starting a new job, I walked around the nursing home to familiarize myself with the units and to meet most of the residents. A homemade sign on one of the doors read, *Jesus Saves.* It stopped me in my tracks. Instantly, a smile came to my face because I thought of the sweet fellowship meeting another believer can bring.

I love to read how Jesus prayed for all believers in John 17:20-26. He prayed to the Father for all of us to be one, just as He and the Father are one. He then prayed for believers to be brought to complete unity to let the world know the Father sent Him. He continued saying, "Righteous Father, I will continue to make You known, so that the love you have for Me may be in them and that I Myself may be in them."

Have you ever noticed how true it is when you meet another Christian, you at once feel like you have known them forever? It has happened many times for me and here was one of those times. This sister in the Lord and I hit it off right away. She lived in a small room on the E-wing unit of a local nursing home.

While telling me her testimony of faith, she shared how she had by herself constructed the *Jesus Saves* sign. Even though this believer was not in her own family house where she wished she could be, she found her contentment in the Lord's Faithfulness and actively followed God's quest to have others there know Him too.

The Lord used me to provide her with fellowship during this time in her life. I imagine it filled in for the lonely times she experienced. I am sure she missed her younger days where she enjoyed independence. God also allowed me to grow in my faith as I watched her be a witness in both Word and deed to the staff and to the other residents.

In displaying our Christian love toward one another, I believe onlookers knew we were Christ's disciples and therefore we honored and glorified God (John 13:35). People who witness the brotherly-love we Christians share will read the recognizable sign saying - *Jesus Saves*.

Prayer: Dear Father God, Jesus prayed for all believers before He went to the cross for us. He prayed for those who believed in Him at the time and for those of us who would eventually believe. My prayer is for many hearts to be open to the message of salvation through Jesus Christ when we as believers display unity amongst each other. The world will know You sent Jesus as Savior and how You love all people when we show oneness in brotherly love. Direct me to someone who needs uplifting and encouragement about Your love for them. In Christ, I pray, Amen.

Meditate on: Romans 1:11-12, Galatians 6:10, Hebrews 10:24-25,

1 Peter 2:17

Gospel Sing – by Cynthia Quattrocelli

Praise the Lord. How good it is to sing praises to our God, how pleasant and fitting to praise Him! Psalm 147:1

Through Jesus, therefore let us continually offer to God a sacrifice of praise-the fruit of lips that confess His name. And do not forget to do good and to share with others, for with such sacrifices God is pleased. Hebrews 13:15-16

Do you believe all people have a God-shaped void in their heart? This is the reason dedicated volunteers tirelessly travel from place to place on a monthly schedule to reach the sick and the elderly with the message of God's Grace. They bring entire singing groups and burst forth with praise songs to the Lord.

I have experienced this proven fact: songs learned in a person's younger days are usually the last thing lost when a person suffers from dementia. More importantly, I have noticed their faith in Christ stands firm. They may not be able to communicate as well, but just watch when the Gospel singers come to lead sing-a-longs at nursing homes. You will see people who usually are known by staff as "nonverbal" begin to sing along with the volunteers. I have seen a calm demeanor come upon the most confused or anxious residents during these gatherings. The sweet Holy Spirit is very present!

The Spiritual teams who travel to skilled nursing facilities hold the hands of the residents and pray for them. These beautiful servants of God are living to fulfill His call by confessing the name of the Lord Jesus Christ to the sick and elderly. Any caregiver can help refresh a person's spiritual roots by being the one to prompt similar activities as described here.

Many verses in the book of Psalms instruct us to sing to the Lord joyfully declaring the works of His hands. Psalm 100:1-2 in the Message Bible exclaims; on your feet now — applaud God! Bring a gift of laughter, sing yourself into His Presence.

Here is a suggestion: in your quiet time with the Lord, start out with reading or singing a Psalm. I have enjoyed doing this for years. The Psalms are beautiful confirmations of God's Love and Faithfulness. Meditating on them can bring quality to your relationship with our Lord. Declaring His attributes of Mercy, Righteousness, Justice, Love, Faithfulness, Goodness, and Strength can grow deep-rooted faith within your heart.

Watch your faith be built-up when reading in the Psalms. See how King David encouraged himself in the Lord and how the Lord sustained him. God is the same yesterday, today, and forever. He truly is worthy of all Honor and Praise. Sing to the Living God (Psalm 89:1).

Prayer: All Mighty God, I sing praises to You and I worship You for Who You Are (Selah). I have no other Gods before me! Righteousness and Justice are the foundation of Your throne; Love and Faithfulness go before You; I walk in the Light of Your Presence, O Lord; I rejoice in Your Name all day long (Psalm 89:14-16). Hallelujah! Father, I come together with other saints to exalt Your Name above the Heavens! And Father, I need Your help daily as I look to You for Wisdom, Revelation, Knowledge, Understanding, and Discernment while giving care to the sick, the lonely, the lost, the young, and the vulnerable. Thank You for working through me to bring Your Goodness to many. In Jesus Name, amen.

Meditate on: 1 Chronicles 16:8-12, Psalm 33, Colossians 3:16, James 5:13-16

Activity Ideas for People with Dementia

Sensory Stroll:

One of my favorite activities to do with folks who have limited abilities is what I call, the "Sensory Stroll."

Inside or outside, I push them in a wheelchair and they experience sensory stimulation by the surrounding environment. Socialization is accomplished when we stop to visit with a passerby.

I like seeing the nursing staff's facial expressions when I ask if I may take certain residents out for a stroll. I like choosing those who have not been outside in months or in years.

The staff then transfers the patient in whatever mobile chair is right for that person's specific needs. They are bundled up with jacket or blanket if it is Spring or Fall.

I have pushed patients in everything from large geriatric chairs to small standard wheelchairs all over the facility grounds. It is well worth the effort when you see the change in the person's countenance and in their increased level of alertness.

These are the folks forgotten many times because of their inability to communicate through verbalization. They just need a chance to shine from within.

Going the Extra Mile – by Cynthia Quattrocelli

Slaves, obey your masters in everything; and do it, not only when their eye is on you and to win their favor, but with sincerity of heart and reverence for the Lord. Whatever you do, work at it with all your heart, as working for the Lord, not for men, since you know that you will receive an inheritance from the Lord as a reward. It is the Lord Christ you are serving. - Colossians 3:22-24

Therefore, my dear brothers, stand firm. Let nothing move you. Always give yourself fully to the work of the Lord, because you know that your labor in the Lord is not in vain. - 1 Corinthians 15:58

There have been times in my life that I remember saying, "I absolutely love working." In fact, I have spoken this truth even the times when I held two jobs. Through my 46 years in the work world, the jobs I held had these titles: Activities Aide, Dementia Care Program Leader, Waitress, Hairdresser, Beauty Shop Owner, Residential Housecleaning Owner/Cleaner, Teacher Assistant, Nanny, Deli Clerk, Dog Groomer, and In-Home Elderly Companion Aide. Through some of those years in the evenings, I also worked a second job as a waitress.

There was a brief time in my employment history after working from 8 am - 6 pm Monday-Friday caring for three children as their fulltime Nanny, (which included cleaning their house, grocery shopping, and cooking) that I also worked full weekends in a pet store as a dog groomer.

God's Word encourages me to do my utmost best in every job. It is what I describe as a calling to care for others in many distinct roles. I give God the glory for the strength and desire to work in the jobs I have held. They came from Him!

I am a shy person, but I have felt God's anointing come on me as soon as I walk into my work assignment. God equipped me with long legs and the energy produced by them. I have been known to be almost running down long nursing home hallways gathering up residents and encouraging them to attend the recreation program I had prepared. Many times, joking residents or staff said, "Slow down, Cindy."

One of the greatest joys I have experienced, is *going the extra mile* for people. My heart would go out to elderly residents when no one was available to help them. Nursing staff are usually attentive, but they get very busy too. I would sense God encouraging me to stop from what I was doing and retrieve a sweater, a cup of water, a walker left behind in their room, etc. I did it out of joy in serving the Lord.

Did you ever consider what you do daily in the workforce can honor Almighty God? Ask the Lord to bless you to have more energy and wisdom to help the anxious or depressed souls you are caring for. Ask Him to help you with certain job responsibilities that prove difficult and to improve your response to them by staying in alignment with His Word.

Whatever situation you are in as caregiver, remember to work as unto the Lord (Colossians 3:24). Do not grow weary in doing good, for in due season you will reap a harvest of good (Galatians 6:9-10). Be a pattern and a model of one who does an excellent job. The God who lives in your heart is a God of excellence!

Prayer: Dear Father God, thank You for entrusting these precious folks in my care. I need strength and wisdom to carry out some of my job duties. Please send someone to help and to encourage me in my work. At times, I do get weary of the heavy responsibilities put on me. I would like to have another Christian sister/brother at my work place. We could lift each other up in prayer and bless each other with Christian fellowship. I know nothing is impossible with you and I thank You for all Your Provision. In the name of Jesus, amen.

Meditate on: Ecclesiastes 4:9, Acts 18:3, Ephesians 4:28, 2 Thessalonians 3:6-13

Obedience Equals Blessings – by Cynthia Quattrocelli

But I tell you: Love your enemies and pray for those who persecute you. -Matthew 5:44

Let your light shine before men, that they may see your good deeds and praise your Father in Heaven. -Matthew 5:16

It had been an enjoyable and productive morning for all in the new Dementia Care Activities Program called, Bridges. The Speech Therapy Manager was overseer and I was hired to be the Coordinator and Activity Leader for the program. This daily small group was held upstairs on the 4th floor. The room had a massive round table just right for activities.

One-day Edith, a resident who lived on the 3rd floor was beaming with self-confidence as she had just finished her appointed task as group leader for that morning. I had called on her to read aloud knowing she still had her reading skills intact. And I felt she needed a little uplifting. Edith had a history of depression. The 3rd floor RN recommended that she be in the group 3-4 times per week to get her away from the isolation of her room. I set out to do my best at engaging the resident in helpful activities to give her more purpose, etc. My aim too was to fulfill the goals the speech therapist wrote for her.

After the first month, her attendance was less than what the goal requested. But for the days that she was present at the group setting, I believe she did enjoy the many activities as evidenced by her level of participation. Since it was a new program and this lady was new at coming, it had been difficult for nursing assistant staff to remember to transfer her to a wheelchair, so I could transport her to/from the dementia program held on the floor above hers. I was willing myself to do the transfers, but I did not have recent training to transfer patients. It was a safety issue.

On this day, Edith was amongst four others who had completed a cognitive-based game. She read aloud names of practical items to have the others match them on their "bingo-type" game boards. I was starting to feel a sense of accomplishment in helping her as I happily documented each resident's response to the activity. During the three hours that passed; she also excelled at a trivia game, recalled family memories, school facts, completed math questions, sang songs from her era, and initiated verbalization. The results amazed me. A joyful fun atmosphere was distinctive each time this new dementia care group was in session. Much was accomplishment that day for this resident and I was happy for her. Edith showed no signs of depression.

Given a chance, people with dementia can gain a sense of self-worth by completing socialization, cognitive, and physical fitness-based tasks.

Eventually, it was time to leave this room and go to lunch. My noon-time routine was to call the nurses' desk on the 3rd floor where Edith lived. I asked to have the Aide assigned to her that day, to come and transfer Edith from the chair she sat in, back into her wheelchair. As with most days, after only a few minutes, all my 4th floor activity residents had left for lunch with the help of their aide. But, I had to wait with Edith until a Nursing Assistant came from Edith's 3rd floor. Finally, at 12:30 a busy but efficient 4th floor assistant came to our rescue, because the 3rd floor Assistant still had not come after a long time of waiting.

After Edith transferred to the wheelchair, I offered to help the Nursing Assistant saying that I could take her in the wheelchair back down to her own floor to eat lunch. As we came off the elevator on the 3rd floor, Edith told me she needed to use the bathroom. I parked her against the wall near the nurse's station. The resident herself called out her need to a staff person who was sitting behind the desk. Thinking she was not heard because no one had answered her and wishing to go the extra mile to help those in my care, I walked up to the nurse's desk and kindly said, "I'm not sure if Edith was heard...she needs help to the bathroom when you get a chance."

A loud nasty-sounding female voice coming from a group of Nursing Assistants standing together not too far from the desk screamed out, "We know, Cindy!" Stunned by the verbal attack, I walked over where the Nursing Assistant was standing. I tried at first, to explain why I had asked for help on behalf of Edith, but after getting harsh words thrown back at me, I walked away. Shaken up a little, I met with my manager later about the incident. She made me feel better, but truthfully, I was fearful of how I would be treated in the coming days.

That evening, I cried out to the Lord about the situation. He reminded me from His Word; I am to forgive others and to love my enemies and pray for those who mistreat me. In Romans 12:17, I followed Paul's teaching; do not repay evil for evil and be careful to do what is right in the eyes of everybody. Once back at work, I applied God's Word toward the situation.

From that day on, each time this staff person was assigned to transport Edith to my program, I said thank you while being sure to address her by her first name. After several weeks, I said to her, "This new program is a success because of nurses like you who help, I couldn't do it without you...thank you." This brought a big smile to her face. From that point on, each time she saw me she was extra helpful to me in my program. *Obedience = Blessings*. It was a blessing for me to hear her call me by my name with a kind tone. In similar circumstances, I have practiced God's direction and have experienced positive results with people. Doing life His way really does bring pleasantness.

God's Word works! It is alive, and He watches over it to carry out what He desires. It does not return to Him void. His way brings peace. Try a little love and see for yourself how it can change the atmosphere. Love your enemies and pray blessings unto them. The thankful words I said to this nurse were true. I did need her help. Do you have some kind words today that the Lord may be prodding you to speak to another person?

Prayer: Father, thank You for the guidance the Word of God brings me for every circumstance I face. It may not be easy for me to forgive and to pray for those who do me wrong. But help me to remember that You love them too. Your Son gave me the Best example when He asked You to forgive the sinner next to Him on the cross and then He added, "for he knows not what he does." Help me Father, for I belong to You through Christ. Help me take seriously the fact that I am called to be an Ambassador for the Kingdom of God. I am to go and win souls. Jesus said that I am salt and light to a dark world. Help me to see things from Your perspective…and then obey and to love my neighbor by being an example of Your Agape Love. In Christ, Amen.

Meditate on: Proverbs 16:7, Romans 12:17-21, 2 Corinthians 5:18-21, Colossians 4:5-6

Lessons with Susie – by Cynthia Quattrocelli

Folly is bound up in the heart of a child, but the rod of discipline will drive it far from him. -Proverbs 22:15

But the fruit of the Spirit is love, joy, peace, patience, kindness, goodness, faithfulness, gentleness, and self-control. -Galatians 5:22

Susie was three years old and the youngest of four siblings when an agency employed me to be the family's full time Nanny. Aware of the children's recent loss of their Mother, I sought out help from God early each morning while they slept upstairs. I would sit at their dining room table reading my Bible. It was the beginning of summer and the kids slept in each day and this allowed quality time for me in the Word.

I had experience caring for children as a Teacher Assistant in day care centers. But this was so different. The two older children were boys and very independent because they were twelve and nine years old. The two girls were not yet school age. It took them awhile to warm up to another woman besides their Mom. After all, I was a stranger in their home. They were not accustomed to seeing anyone but Mom cooking in their kitchen. But, we all did enjoy happy times when I was reading their favorite books to them or taking walks together.

Occasionally, I had to put Susie in the time-out chair for three minutes (one minute per age) to help her learn to listen and follow through with the directions I would give. It was tough because I wanted to just pick her up to cuddle and allow her to get away with stuff. She was acting out because of missing her Mom. But, I knew it would be important for this young child to learn how to listen and obey teachers when she was ready for school.

One day, she was so mad she kicked me as I passed by her. In stubbornness, her fanny was half off and half on the time-out chair. On that day and others like them, it was difficult to not let anger take over in my heart toward her. Little by little though, she and I became close. When the four older children went off to school in September, we spent quality time together as I polished Susie's nails, curled her hair, took her to visit with other kids, and to the library for the children's reading hour. I was learning patience and unconditional love.

As we see in 1 Corinthians 13:4-5, love is patient, kind, and not easily angered. Now, I am not saying that I have arrived at a point in my life where I never have anger flare up in me. God continues His suitable work in me. I thank the Lord that He used this situation of *lessons with Susie* and other similar experiences to develop in me a love for people. I often ask Him this; Lord help me to get a little closer at loving people more like You do.

You can be confident of this in your role as a helper; "that He who began a good work in you will carry it on to completion until the day of Christ Jesus" (Philippians 1:6).

Prayer: Our Loving Father God, I praise the Name of Jesus! I'm aware of how You are training me to live a righteous life for Your Glory. Therefore, help me to be an example to the children in my life in a way where they will want to honor You. Remind me to be a good listener and a doer of the Word which You have planted in me. When I come around a negative person, I will pray for Your help remembering to be patient and loving; help me to expect how You desire a circumstance to turn out. Lord, when I plant seeds of forgiveness, show me a harvest of good growing from them. In Jesus' Name, Amen.

Meditate on: Proverbs 8:17, Book of James, 1 John 3:11-24

"Dziekuje!" (thank you) – by Cynthia Quattrocelli

Praise be to the God and Father of our Lord Jesus Christ, the Father of compassion and the God of all comfort, who comforts us in all our troubles, so that we can comfort those in any trouble with the comfort we ourselves have received from God. - 2 Corinthians 1:3-4

Cast all your anxiety on Him for He cares for you. -1 Peter 5:7

Harriet is frightened - her daughter told me. Observing Harriet in the first few days after her family moved her from her own home in suburbia to this city nursing home, I could see it was scary for her. She was away from what had been familiar to her for decades. Here at this facility she was assigned to share a small room with a stranger; another elderly woman. Her own private space in this shared room was probably the same size her bathroom had been at her own home.

Harriet's family were making the choices for her these days. Harriet suffered from moderate Dementia, and this means that her short-term memory was impaired and she had limited reasoning ability. Folks with dementia are usually attacked with depression as well. This was the case for my friend, Harriet. Fortunately, she had a very attentive family who took turns visiting her daily.

Thank goodness, her adjustment at our facility was supported because her room was right next to the small lounge where I held dementia activity programs Monday through Friday. This allowed me to befriend Harriet and to help her. Many times, late in the afternoon when activity programs were over and during the typical "sun-downing" time, she often would self-propel herself in the wheelchair up and down the long hallways calling out her daughter's name.

Sun-downing is a term that caretakers use to describe the late afternoon change in behavior for residents with dementia. Wandering, increased anxiousness, or combativeness are typical symptoms of sun-downing. What I have proven successful when trying to calm such residents in my care is to simply sit with them just holding their hand. Harriet always calmed down with this individual attention. Redirection works too. We enjoyed completing water coloring projects together before dinner. And it was rewarding for me to help her at meal times when she declined to the point of not wanting to eat anything but sweets. She was my friend.

One day, during a quiet time, I asked her to help me learn how to say, "thank you" in her Grandmother's Polish language. *"Dziekuje" (Jen KOO yeh)* is what she taught me to say. During this lesson, I had a bird's eye view of a younger Harriet without all the troubles she was now battling every day. As she taught me the Polish greeting, I saw contentment in her eyes. For a moment, she was a young Mom again teaching her daughter.

After about three months of living in her unfamiliar environment, it was noticeable that Harriet started to consider me as a "lifeline." If she would see me from a distance down the hall, she scrambled up the hallway in her wheelchair with arm raised high calling out what she thought was my name. She never got my name correct, but it did not matter. At times, she would be crying and I knew I had to re-introduce the comfort of God's love when she appeared so helpless and hopeless.

I like the verse in Philippians 4:7 that promises us the peace of God which transcends all understanding, guarding our hearts and minds in Christ Jesus, if we make our requests known to Him. At those times when she displayed hopelessness, I attempted to bring her back to any relationship she may have had with the Lord by reminding her of the price He paid for her salvation. I spoke about doing her part which was to receive the Lord's Grace by faith.

When I would present this hope to those in my care, I did not always see a distinct faith, but our Savior knows who believes. My role is to follow the way of love as I visit and comfort the sick and the lonely and carry the Gospel to them. The rest is in His Capable Hands. He tells us, "Be still and know that I am God." (Psalm 46:10)

Prayer: Dear Father of All Comfort, I know You give Love and Care to all You have made (Psalm 145). I am blessed by the promises in the Word telling me to rejoice in the Lord always and with prayer and petition along with thanksgiving I will receive Peace in my heart. My hope is for Your Peace to enter the heart of ___ (put a name here), who is in my care. Help me Lord as I aim to show gentleness to them; I know You are near. Thank You for the chance to share Your Love with all people. Regarding those who I regularly help; I do recognize the Love You've been steadily planting in my heart for them. Bless them with more of You. In Jesus' Name, Amen.

Meditate on: Psalm 145:17-20, Proverbs 3:5-6, Romans 15:13,

1 Thessalonians 5:18.

The Church Lady – by Cynthia Quattrocelli

Remember your Creator in the days of your youth, before the days of trouble come and the years approach when you will say, "I find not pleasure in them." - Ecclesiastes 12:1

Jesus said to her, "I am the Resurrection and the life. He who believes in me will live even though he dies."- John 11:25

Elsie, was a woman cared for by nurses and by her own family. Her sisters described her as having been very active in her church. She had been a Deacon. As with all the other residents in the home where I worked, I aimed at finding out about her past leisure time interests. I planned then to provide recreation therapy in the best way possible. This provision was even attempted for those in a coma or who were unable to speak. Elsie fit this category. She was alive and breathing, but unresponsive. She had lived like this for three years before I had come to work there. Her skin was radiant looking, but her eyes never opened. Nursing staff gave Elsie the best skilled care.

The family visited weekly and fussed over Elsie's hair and applied lotion to her skin. They appeared to be having good times of Christian fellowship while sitting in chairs around their sister's bed. I thought it was wonderful how they still included her in their family gatherings. Relatives were coming to "her home" there, just as they might have if she were well and in her own house on Cherry Street.

On their frequent visits, the sisters prayed for her while altogether. I am sure they did the same in their own homes and at her Church congregation. This was a beloved *church lady* whose name was brought up to God, often.

During the times I visited, I spoke to her as if her eyes were open and she was showing attention to what I said. I read scripture verses aloud, played Gospel music on the tape player, and held her hand.

Years passed by. One day, I prayed right there alongside her bed. I said, "Lord, thank You for having mercy on Elsie and blessing her with the hope of the new life You paid for her to have. Thank You for this time her sisters are spending with her. I thank You for the promise that someday in Your right timing, she will go on to her reward with You in Heaven."

We did see that glorious day come for the Church lady. Elsie was released to her Creator and Savior. In God's great mercy, He took her home where the Bible tells us there is no more sickness, no pain, no crying. We believe God answered the sister's prayers and my cry for His right timing. "Precious in the sight of the Lord is the death His saints" (Psalm 116:15).

Prayer: Thank You Lord because our present sufferings are not worth comparing with the Glory that will be revealed to us. You who search our hearts know the mind of the Spirit and the Spirit intercedes for the saints in accordance with God's will. "Let us always be mindful to offer up prayer for our brethren everywhere" (Romans 8:18-27). In Jesus' name, Amen.

Meditate on: Matthew 7:7-8, Romans 8:18-27, 2 Corinthians 4:16-18, 2 Corinthians 5:1-10

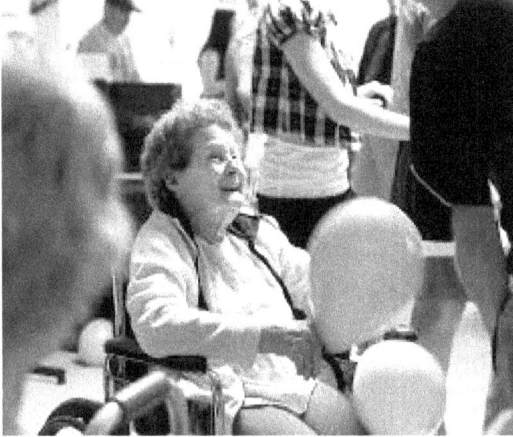

A

cheerful heart

is

good medicine,

but

a crushed spirit

dries up

the bones.

Proverbs 17:22

Holy Spirit Equipped – by Cynthia Quattrocelli

May the favor of the Lord God rest upon us; establish the works of our hands for us- yes, establish the works of our hands. - Proverbs 90:17

For it is God who works in you to will and to act according to His good purpose. - Philippians 2:13

Every day when I walked into the nursing home I felt the familiar Power from on high to help me assist and love the residents there. I was a different person when I came into their midst. I knew His Direction for the tasks I needed to achieve. It was like Jesus talking to the needy elderly using my mouth and His Sweet Presence to show them how He cared about them. I could feel His energy kick in as I sped through the units gathering wheel-chair bound folks to take them to the recreation activities I had planned. I sure was glad for my sneakers to run two steps at a time in the stairwells going from floor to floor in this long-term care facility.

Holy Spirit equipped, I completed tasks at this exhilarating rate. It was quicker to use the stairs than wait for the one and only elevator. I wanted to include residents from all four floors and units for my activity programs. I wheelchair transported a sizeable number of people to wait at the elevator door on one floor. Then I took four folks at a time on it to the right floor. I repeated this process for each floor. Finally, I fetched the folks who lived on the same floor where the activity would take place.

That was only the beginning. Once they were there, I proceeded to explain the program and to help and guide each resident to achieve their optimal participation level. My goal always was to have the activity serve as a way of maintaining their daily living skills.

God does establish the work of our hands. He gives us strength for the tasks we do daily. As a wife and a caregiver, I love the lively words in Proverbs 31:10-31 illustrating the wife of noble character: "She sets about her work vigorously; her arms are strong for her tasks; she opens her arms to the poor and extends her hands to the needy."

Those verses describe beautifully those who serve the Lord as caregivers. He has planned for you to do this. Others are called to other things. I have had people tell me they would never have the patience to work in a nursing home. I smile and say, "Oh, but it's fun." It is a privilege to be called for the purpose God designed and prepared you to do.

"God is very close to the widow, the orphan, and to the brokenhearted" (Psalm 34 and 68). Thank Him because He chose you to be like Him and to be His hands and feet. I have loved God's calling for me to care for the elderly. It is particularly fulfilling to rally around and to help sustain those who suffer from the impacts of dementia.

Prayer: Heavenly Father, thank You for how You prepare us to care for the sick and lonely. I know You are my Strength and You support me daily in the calling You have selected for my life. I am clothed for the job with vitality and self-esteem. Your Power is made perfect in my weakness. I praise You and believe You are the Source I profit from every day to love, and to encourage those I have extended my hands to help. Continue to meet me where I am lacking, in Jesus Name, Amen.

Meditate on: Proverbs 31, Isaiah 40:29-31, Romans 15:1, Philippians 4:13

Thank God for Volunteers – by Cynthia Quattrocelli

Two are better that one for their work produces a better return - Ecclesiastes 4:9

Bear one another's burdens, and so fulfill the law of Christ -Galatians 6:2

I am grateful for wonderful volunteers which helped in diverse ways at the facilities I have worked in. These people could have stayed home on cold wintry days or even on sunny beach-calling days, but instead they chose to come and give their service to help others.

Bingo, arts & crafts, active games, and music programs always went more smoothly when I had the help of a volunteer. In any setting, you will find several residents needing one-on-one help due to their visual, hearing, or physical limitations. In my experience, when a volunteer sat with a challenged resident, it freed me up to apply more creative measures to bring the fulfillment of a higher level of participation from the others. Therefore, every resident in the program was better able to accomplish their optimal level of participation.

At sing-a-longs, we transported a greater number of residents when we had these helpers on the floor. This support found Activity staff achieving our measured goals for residents who had sensory and social needs to fulfill by the State's standards.

The activity programs having a higher attendance due to the volunteer's service also added to the nursing staff success in completing their required tasks on time. Because more residents got out of their rooms to go to the activities with the help of volunteers, it freed up Nurse's Aides to make beds, care for the bed-bound, or to take a needed break.

To on-lookers, it may seem like a simple thing to volunteer. Those who do not work in a nursing home or in a similar care-based setting may think the help is not needed. But, we do need their help. I was determined to have some good helpers, so I decided to take it upon myself and by advertising in a local paper and putting up signs for volunteers at a Senior Center. I was yearning for more help in my Dementia Activities Program. I truly wanted the activity events I had worked so hard on, to succeed. And for this, I needed more hands.

When one truly dedicates himself to helping another, he is honoring God and His Word. In Isaiah 58:6-11, God identifies true fasting as satisfying the needs of the oppressed. There is a promise attached to this as well. He says, then I will guide you always and satisfy your needs in a sun-scorched land and strengthen your frame.

I remember times at my post as a caregiver when I came to the Lord in prayer asking for a specific kind of volunteer to help and asking for God to direct another believer to come to work where I was. He always came through for me. Remember; Moses had Aaron!

How about you. Will you help? There is an abundant need for volunteers. You will be following God's guidelines for considering others by looking to their interests and not only to your own (Philippians 2:4). Thank you.

Prayer: Dear Father, bless volunteers who unselfishly give time and talent to help those in need. I pray for an added number of retired folks to help by using their skills to bless others at nursing homes, prisons, schools, etc. I pray that they will realize how rewarding volunteering is. And Lord, remind me to honor them by saying, thank you. In Jesus Name, Amen.

Meditate on: Proverbs 11:24, Acts 20:35, 1 Timothy 6:17-19,

1 Peter 4:10

Look for the Silver-Lining – by Cynthia Quattrocelli

Live in harmony with one another. Do not be proud, but be willing to associate with people of low position. Do not be conceited. -Romans 13:16

My brothers, as believers in our glorious Lord Jesus Christ, do not show favoritism. -James 2:1

Judy was a new resident to the assisted living facility where I worked as the Dementia Care Activities Leader. She used a walker and was a lady with a witty character. Staff filled me in with what they thought was relevant for me to know about this resident since she would soon be in my activity group - a club for people with dementia.

Most staff there felt she did not belong in this assisted living setting due to her cognitive level resulting in some bad grooming problems. They reasoned how she should have been placed in a nursing home instead. Her daughter was not ready to do that. When I first saw her, I was happy to notice her joyful smile and bright eyes welcoming me to stay and visit. Judy was quick to laugh and joke around with all those close by seeking to get their attention. I enjoyed befriending this cute and bubbly personality.

Each day, she was ready and waiting in the front reception area for someone to come along and visit with her. Most residents shunned her because of her untidiness especially since they had already studied her table manners in the dining room. Several times, kitchen staff had to move her to a new table assignment because someone complained how she was eating with her fingers or because she took another person's food or drink by accident. I made it my plan to be the one at lunch and dinner time to take her right to her seat. I used a handy wipe to wash her fingers before eating. I always put her glass straight in front of her and told her this was her drink. An OT therapist tried to help her to regain her skills at using a fork, but it did not help. She had regressed back to a child in some ways.

I have continuously strived at seeing the good in all people and of course there was good in Judy too. I observed her encouraging people to laugh and she would each time say, "I like to see people laugh and have fun." She loved playing a powerful game of balloon volleyball around the table with several ladies in the dementia activity club. In her earlier years, she had been a good artist and was very lovely in her appearance.

Judy taught me her favorite song, *"Look for the Silver-Lining"* (written by B. G. De Sylva). Many times, she and I joyfully sang it for the others in our little group. Judy got a kick out of holding the last note longer than need be just to hear everyone laugh. This was her goal. Each time, she let the last note finally fade away, she then commented how she had made us all laugh. As months passed, I grew to love her and wanted to protect her from the nasty remarks and haughty treatment from other residents. Even some of the personnel staff did not show her patience.

As you work in the job of a caregiver, consider God's Word. In the book of James, it says, you are doing right when you love your neighbor as yourself. Make it a new resolution to investigate the good that is in everyone. Just as in the words of Judy's favorite song direct the listener to look for the silver-lining whenever clouds appear in the blue, we are to look for the value within everyone while on our watch. It was as if the song Judy continually sang invited those around her to take time for discovering hidden treasures in her heart.

When you show love and kindness, it not only brings out the best in others, but good will come back to you too. If some do not accept it, then love them anyway, for this is the will of God (Mark 12:31).

I included Judy in activity programs I knew were too difficult for her, but she wanted to attend because I was leading them. Therefore, I encouraged her against the advice of other staff associates. Because she had learned to identify me as a person she could trust, she'd follow me around even when I had other duties to do, such as helping higher-functioning residents.

One day, she searched me out and found me way on the other side of the building taking library books to another resident's room. I decided now was the time I wanted to guide her in a prayer to call upon the Lord. She so sweetly repeated the Gospel prayer right there in the hallway. I am not sure if this was her own faith speaking, but I know God is faithful and He will take it from there.

"Thanks be to God, who always leads us in triumphal procession in Christ and through us spreads everywhere the fragrance of the knowledge of Him" (2 Corinthians 2:14).

Prayer: Father God, I am grateful for people who make us smile and laugh. Thank You for giving us music, art, sports, creative ideas, and unique personalities all of which bring us enjoyment while here on earth. Most importantly though, I thank You for Your Son who came and took our place on the cross. He redeemed us from the curse of death. Praise God! Lord Jesus, help me as a caregiver be dedicated in serving You. Help me to purposely commend the good in everyone. Your Love oozing out of us will draw people to You. Help me to be in tune with Your leading to guide souls towards faith in You. In Jesus Name, Amen.

Meditate on: Mark 10:31, Galatians 5:22-23, 1 Timothy 21:15, James 2, 1 Peter 2:1-25

"Why is Everything About Jesus?" -Cynthia Quattrocelli

In everything, set them an example by doing what is good. -Titus 2:7

But just as you excel in everything-in faith, in speech, in knowledge, in complete earnestness and in your love for us-see that you also excel in this grace of giving. -2 Corinthians 8:7

Working as a Nanny, I felt I could and should be an example of Christ to these children. They were in my care for ten hours a day for five days a week. I was glad to have God as my Helper to care for and guide these kids.

I clung to Jesus in a new way back then because He had recently delivered me from a root of bitterness. I was so thankful. Now, faith for my heart's desire to happen was more secure after resentment left. I committed myself to show my parents love and honor out of obedience to the Lord. In fact, this was His direct assignment after deliverance from this sin. I wanted His blessings. I obeyed His personal command. He said, "now, go plant good seed."

This began my quest to believe Him to bless me with a man after God's own heart. Marriage was something I had always hoped for, but never felt good enough to receive. But this release brought out a hidden hope within me. I was free from the lies of the enemy. He had convinced me for years that it would never happen for me. Now my faith level was high for my heart's desire to come.

Now in this newer walk with Christ, I faithfully went back to church after being away for nine years. This was a sunny time in my life. My plans glowed with a new Light. The Holy Spirit refreshed me. I started attended a weekly Bible study and found Christian friends in a singles group. Daily, I was falling more in with love with Jesus! Even though I had been saved for over thirteen years, the recent radical repentance with time spent on my face crying out to Him, changed my life forever. This was indeed a turning-point.

The Lord spoke often to me as I sought Him with all my heart. In Jeremiah 29:13, God says, "If you seek Me with all your heart, I will be found by you." I heard His still small voice. An inner witness said, "Lovely, Lovable, and Loving." I knew instantly He was showing me what qualities make a good wife, but these are also recognizable as His own character traits of excellence. He was developing in me: the fruits of the Spirit.

Now, back to the kids that I was caring for, they probably thought of me as weird. They heard me thank God for everything just out of the joy in my heart. I did not force the Bible at them. I lived it by example. I cared for them in a loving way and in a fair manner. We had good times together. I kept my composure and prayed to be patient if they did not follow the directions designed by their parents, etc. I wanted to be an example of God's love.

One day, the oldest child who was a teenager at the time asked me in a sarcastic tone, *"Why is everything about Jesus?"* I answered respectfully, "Because it is!"

"I Am the Alpha and the Omega," says the Lord God, "who is, and who was, and who is to come, the Almighty" (Revelation 1:8). The Lord warns us by saying; "Whoever acknowledges Me before men, I will also acknowledge him before My Father in Heaven. But whoever disowns Me before men, I will disown him before My Father in Heaven" (Matthew 10:32-33).

I pray for the caregivers reading this by using Apostle Paul's words, "I pray that your love may abound more and more in knowledge and depth of insight, so that you may be able to discern what is best and may be pure and blameless until the day of Christ, filled with the fruit of righteousness that comes through Jesus Christ to the glory and praise of God" (Philippians 1:9-10).

Today, my testimony of waiting for the right husband is complete. The Lord used me to plant Good seed into those young ones who were in my care for three years. God not only develops us during our seasons of waiting, He uses our faith stance to help others look to Him. The result of my Divine anticipation manifested and God received the Glory.

Prayer: Lord God, You are so Good! "You answer the cry of the lonely and you set them in families" (Psalm 68:6). You have a "plan of good" designed for each one - Jeremiah 29:11. I pray that while I am giving care, I will be expecting Your Presence every day to show up at my work place. Use me to help people of all ages to know how real, alive, and active You are. I need Your Divine intervention to enable me to work at allowing love, patience, wisdom, and discernment into my care routine. As it says in Philippians 4:13, "I can do everything through Christ who strengthens me." In Jesus Name, Amen.

Meditate on: Psalm 119:160, Luke 18:27, 2 Corinthians 1:10-11,

1 Peter 2:9

A Cheerful Giver – by Cynthia Quattrocelli

"Love the Lord your God with all your heart and with all your soul and with all your strength, and with all your mind, and love your neighbor as yourself."- Luke 10 27

He who is kind to the poor lends to the Lord, and He will reward him for what he has done. - Proverbs 19:17

Love described in 1 John 3:16-17 is this: "knowing Jesus Christ laid down His life for us." The remaining words to this verse show us what our part is for giving love: "and we ought to lay down our lives for our brothers. If anyone has material possessions and sees his brothers in need but has no pity him, how can the love of Christ be in him."

The sign read, "Free Community Dinner Every Thursday Evening." After work one day, I drove past this invitation posted out front of a church. The area was a low-income neighborhood. I reflected on how the Lord had just recently blessed me with a substantial pay increase. And, with this new wage I paid larger amounts toward my debt. It was great to afford more groceries too. What a huge financial miracle it was for me when I was chosen at work to be the coordinator for a new program. With it came a $ 7.00/hour pay increase. Praise the Lord! Now, I wanted to help others by using my financial blessing.

Studying the sign on the lawn, I felt drawn to this new ministry to feed the poor in our city. Soon after, on each Thursday instead of going home from work, I arrived at this church in time to help set up the dining room and then greet the neighborhood when they came in to have a meal with us. It blessed my heart when paying for some of the cost of ingredients, but helping to serve the food was a what I enjoyed doing most. I loved serving the people there. It was nice to have the chance to sit and eat with those who would otherwise have been alone at a table. I had hoped they would benefit from a sense of "family".

I incorporated this new endeavor into my 9-5 job helping elderly folks. So, on my planned activities calendars, I added some purposeful community-based programs. Arrangements were for the nursing home residents to fill Easter baskets as gifts for the poor children coming to the church weekly for the free meals. My elderly activity program participants loved hearing about how the children delighted in the treats they had so lovingly prepared for them. Another time, volunteers came with me as I took a group of our Senior Shoppers in the facility van to the dollar store at Christmas time. We helped the residents choose items to send oversees to kids in underdeveloped countries. They had a grand time picking out toys and essentials to pack into shoeboxes for the Samaritan's Purse Christmas Shoebox Ministry (www.samaritanspurse.org).

I have discovered over the years while giving care, it lifts my spirits when I do something good for someone else. Many a day, I did not feel at all like going to work. I was living in an area where there was a lot of snow and many cloudy days. Cold wintry days can make you want to stay home. Although, when I arrived at my job and saw how the Lord was drawing me to help a resident in need, this was when I got a lift out of a bad-day feeling.

Make it a point to see where you can serve God's people and in doing so it will bring many expressions of thanks to God. Hebrews 13:16 says, "and do not forget to do good and to share with others, for with such sacrifices, God is pleased." My sharing with others, at the time, was the Thursday night dinners, Easter baskets, and shoeboxes to fill up. These opportunities brought me a chance to be *a cheerful giver* which overflowed in many expressions of thanks to God (2 Corinthians 9:7-12).

Prayer: Father God, Thank You for all my blessings. You are able to make all grace abound to me, so that in all things, at all times, having all that I need, I will abound in every good work. You love a cheerful giver and supply seed for the sower and bread for food, therefore enlarging the harvest of Your righteousness. I am made rich in every way so that I can be generous on every occasion, and through my generosity, the result is thanksgiving to You. Help me to believe and then see Your hand providing for resources to help the poor. In Jesus Name, amen.

Meditate on: Psalm 140:12, 2 Corinthians 8:1-24, Ephesians 4:28, Philippians 2:4

But the fruit of the Spirit is love,

joy, peace, patience,

kindness, goodness, faithfulness,

gentleness, and self-control.

Against such things,

there is no law.

Galatians 5:22-23

A Place to Stay – by Cynthia Quattrocelli

Share with God's people who are in need. Practice hospitality. -Romans 12:13

God sets the lonely in families -Psalm 68:6

I cherished the single women's group I was a part of. A best friend of mine, Arlene and another single Christian, Cecelia started the group. The two merged their ideas for a group when they first met after a church service one day. Cecelia (then a single Mom) said to herself during the service, "Today if no one stops to say hello to me in church, I am going to start my own single women's group." The Lord heard Cecelia's heart and directed Arlene to say hi to this sister in the Lord. In talking, they discovered they were both single. Each of them were believing the Lord for a Godly man to marry. They laughed at how God must have certainly planned for them to meet because they each had similar ideas of starting a Christian fellowship group for single women.

Plans took shape and they decided to name their group, H.U.G.G.S.S. It stands for, Handmaidens Used to Guide God's Single Sisters. This group was a lifeline for me during my lonely Single years as I waited for God to prepare me for the right mate.

One day at a monthly meeting, I met Barb who had come for the first time to our H.U.G.G.S. group. She had a bubbly personality! Because she considered me to be her sister in the Lord, even though we had only just met at this meeting, she offered me a ride home. I did not have a car back then. When she dropped me off she said, "Cindy If you ever need a place to stay, let me know - You can stay with me." Her generosity shocked me. After I got out of the car, I thought to myself, I will be okay. I had hopes of doing financially better soon.

During this time in my life, I was just making ends meet. The back debt I owed did not help matters. I only had a part time job and was searching for another job to make up the difference. Several months later after Barb's kind offer, I did indeed have to call her out of desperation. I was not finding full time work and so I could not keep up with my rent payment. The Lord knew ahead of time I was going to need a roommate. Our Heavenly Father really does know our needs before we even ask (Matthew 6:32). I am so thankful to God for this brief time of respite while living with Barb. We transformed her dining room into my bedroom. I worked doing a few cleaning jobs for income and she allowed me to use her car. Our agreement included me cleaning her house and doing the gardening to pay for my room and board.

Being Barb's roommate was a restful time in my life. In the previous twelve years, I had worked two jobs at times, to help my biological sister (a single Mom) support her kids. Now, I was sensing the Lord allowing me more time in His Word and a closer intimacy with my Creator. I stayed with my friend Barb for ten months and then God opened the door to a fulltime job. With this new position, I could now afford my own apartment and begin again.

During those months in getting to know Barb (who was a retired RN), I found out she also had a generous heart toward others. I was not the only one she had taken in. She told me of several small families she had allowed to live with her till eventually they could afford to live on their own. Barb was a new believer too and was zealous for the Lord. I guess she caught on quickly to the golden rule. Christ taught it. He said, "So in everything, do to others what you would have them do to you, for this sums up the law and the prophets" (Matthew 7:12). Having been a Nurse, Barb was a caring soul. Fondly, I think back to her generosity.

She followed the way of love when giving me *a place to stay*. Her example encourages me to inspect my life and then boost my own efforts at becoming more supportive as a Christian, neighbor, friend, and caregiver.

Prayer: Heavenly Father, I thank You for the people or situations in my life that have been instrumental in my moving ahead to a better situation. I know You put them in place to help me. I embrace this wonderful truth too: once we are saved by God's grace through Christ, we have the promised Holy Spirit as our ultimate Helper. My prayer is that I will recognize many God-created moments and encounters, while I'm supplying an extra hand to the helpless in my care. Lord, my desire is to live by Your Word and to love and help others as You have commanded me to do. In Jesus Name, Amen.

Meditate on: Acts 4:32-35, Titus 1:8, James 1:27, 1 Peter 4:9-10

No More Tears, No More Pain, No More Wheelchairs
- by Cynthia Quattrocelli

He will wipe away every tear from their eyes. There will be no more death or mourning or crying or pain, for the old order of things has passed away. He who is seated on the throne said, "I am making everything new!" -Revelation 21:4-5

"Do not let your hearts be troubled. Trust in God; trust also in Me. In My Father's house are many rooms; if it were not so, I would have told you. I am going to prepare a place for you." -John 14:1-2

Paula was a sweet lady who lived in one of the nursing homes I had worked in as an Activity Leader. She was paralyzed on one side due to a stroke. Thankfully, she had the ability to speak and make her needs known. I transported her via wheelchair to her chosen activity programs. Her favorite was bingo, although she was willing to try any activity we offered even ones that required for us to do most of the activity for her. I always considered her as a humble person. She tried her best to complete arts and crafts projects. I believe she was really trying to make the best of her situation. Paula always giggled at one of our staff person's silly antics. From another room, everyone working there recognized her chuckling laugh. Staff liked her a lot. Paula also seemed to enjoy the individual talks she had with us.

Often, when I was cleaning up after a program, she stayed and shared hope of her family coming to visit or we just talked about any subject that came up. In one visit, she asked me to confirm to her again what she had heard someone tell her about Heaven. She said, "I heard that in Heaven, there is no sickness or pain." I answered her by stating what I had remembered in the book of Revelation 21:4. I said, "Yes Paula, you are right and that means you will not be in a wheelchair in Heaven! You can look forward to *no more tears, no more pain, and no more wheelchairs.* You will walk and run and be forever with the Lord." I was happy to recite this verse to her about no more death, or mourning or crying or pain, for the old order of things had passed. God gave us a New Covenant.

When at work, it was wonderful to have a Christian resident to converse with and to share in agreement about the Love of God. It is sad when you see others who do not care to trust in the Lord. So, Paula was refreshing. I can still hear her laughter. It sounded more like a cackle. We all loved her dearly.

Be thankful for little strides. Look for open doors to share God's love. The Truth of eternal hope through Christ is the ultimate in caregiving. Sometimes the grind of daily routines can replace our required compassion for individuals who are in our care. If you are in this condition, before beginning a day as a caregiver, start out by undergoing a love exchange with our Heavenly Father.

His love goes before you (Psalm 89:14). Fathom who God is by collecting names associated with His character. For example: Righteous, Faithful, Goodness, Steadfast, All Sufficient One, Lover of my soul, Giver of Good Gifts, etc. He reveals Himself in His written Word. When you become more aware of who He is, faith rises to ask Father God how you can bring some joy, laughter, and hope to the person you are helping. Pray for God to help you to see good things in people who act bad-tempered. I truly believe there is good in all people. After all, they are made in His image and - God is good.

A missionary friend once guided. She said that God gently told her, He only asks us to simply "lift" others up in prayer. To the dear caregiver reading this: lift-up the names of the ones, who you bring relief to. Lift them up to God.

Prayer: Dear Goodness, how awesome are the plans You have for me and for those You allow me to love and oversee. I thank You for using caregivers to show Your love and comfort to the hurting people in this world. Enable me through the Holy Spirit to encourage and to confirm the faith of people who are looking forward to the great promise of eternal life. With Your help, show me open doors to guide the ones who do not know You yet. I pray they will come to You, in Jesus Name, Amen.

Meditate on: 1Corinthians 2:9, Hebrews 13:14, 2 Peter 3:13

Great is Thy Faithfulness – by Cynthia Quattrocelli

This is the day that the Lord has made; let us rejoice and be glad in it. - Psalm 118:24

If we are faithless, He will remain faithful, for He cannot disown Himself. -2nd Timothy 2:13

The years of loss, loneliness, or financial struggle can splinter our lives. But, we may look back to see them as the sweetest we have had on earth. It is probable, that in those seasons, we were more desperate in our search to discover the caring nature of our Faithful Lord.

During my many years as a single woman, it was always consoling for me to sing to the Lord while walking home from work. As soon as my feet touched the sidewalk, I yielded my heart in melody to Him. Quietly, I sang the hymn, *Great Is Thy Faithfulness*. The words ministered to me as I sung about His goodness. They built a strong connection between me and the Lord and provided me with His Peace. Although in my mid-thirties, I was only a youngster in the Lord - in a spiritual grade school. His Word nurtured me as I discovered His character of steadfastness and faithfulness.

Father God was teaching me many things and healing frayed corners of my heart. I have come to believe; It was God Himself who started singing in my heart as soon as my feet hit the pavement on my walks home. Now, some mornings upon awakening, an ongoing worship song begins a performance in my heart the moment my eyes welcome the new day. While basking in the truth of His mercies when I sang to Him, I was acquiring an Abba Father (Daddy) relationship with the God of All. He is always in the role of a Caregiver.

The hymn speaks to hearts saying - each morning, noon, and night and every season, my Father cares for me. As I sang this through the years of my growth in the Lord Jesus, I grew to trust and confirm His Consistent Presence. He was telling me, all is well and He is Faithful to deliver all the support I need.

The Lord melted my heart with a knowing that someday I will be doing a different work for His glory. I was not to be concerned about where I was then. I learned to trust Him for all my tomorrows. He spoke to me. He said, "The Repairer of Broken Dreams."

Decide to hang out with Him anywhere and anytime. I can tell you this; He makes it well worth the time spent with Him. It is not about how many verses you read or how elaborate your prayers are. He has called you to receive the kingdom of God like a little child (Luke 18:17). A humble childlike relationship with Your Savior directs and deepens the walk you have with God the Father. *Great is Thy Faithfulness!*

Prayer: Father God, help me to know You in the same way a little child does, who has a loving Papa. Comfort me, as You develop faith in me to know and to believe You are always there for me and nothing is too hard for You (Jeremiah 32:27). I declare Your written Word over my life and that It will prove life-changing for me. Teach me to speak Your Word over situations instead of only reporting the negative things trying to overtake me. Abba Father, I know the plans You have for me are good because You are good. Thanks again, for the Best of Care, in Jesus Name. Amen.

Meditate on: Proverbs 10:28, Lamentations 3:21-26, Romans 5:22

The Walking Club – by Cynthia Quattrocelli

*She sets about her work vigorously; her arms are strong for her tasks.
–Proverbs 31:17*

*Do you not know that in a race all the runners run, but only one gets
the prize? -1Corinthians 9:24*

Walking outside was so appreciated by a few of the elderly who could still move right along without assistance. In *the walking club*, I enjoyed taking these folks around the entire assisted living building. Some of the people were independent to go it alone, but I was responsible as the Activities Assistant to stay with those at risk for falls and wandering.

This program was specifically beneficial for Martha. We walked twice daily to promote tiredness, so she would not elope and have everyone in the place out looking for her. She could really talk up a storm too. If any of you have ever helped a person with dementia, you will understand how their repetitive questions or comments can wear on you. The person is not aware they just said the same thing moments before. I patiently listened as she asked the same questions about my family on each of our walks together.

I answered each question using the same words I used the last time she had asked it, only minutes before. I too inquired about her family to spark reminiscing. Amazement struck me when after four months into this daily walking and talking routine, she initiated true statements about my family. Amazingly, Martha had heard my answers enough times to remember them. I had been told Martha had a diagnosis of dementia with short-term memory impairment. Never the less, she retained information because someone cared to take time consistently to talk with her.

I marveled at how she started each day with vigor for life, just as verses from the Bible teach us about being diligent in all we do. Nothing seemed to stop her from enjoying the life God had given her to live. This woman's approach to life and her interest about my family reminded me of how Philippians 2:14-16 teaches us to "not only look to our own interests, but also to the interests of others."

Our attitude should be the same as Christ's. We are to do everything without complaining or arguing, becoming blameless Children of God and shine like the stars in the universe as we hold out the Word of Life. Let us not run, walk, or labor for nothing, but let us continue our calling as loving Christ-like caregivers in an environment hungry for hope. Faith in Jesus Christ brings eternal Hope (Hebrews 12:1-3).

Prayer: Father God, I am glad for every day that brings me fulfillment as I assist others in a manner worthy of You. It is a pleasure indeed to serve my loving God with what seems like trivial things such as, simply being a good listener. Bless other caregivers too, for I know that You are enabling all of us to keep on running the good race. You have placed us where we are. Empower each one to run while carrying the Gospel of Christ's Light, Life, and Love to the hopeless. Teach us to have the attitude and eternal love for others as Christ desires, for thy will be done on earth as it is in Heaven. We petition Your help and seek You with all our hearts. I know You will be found by us. Amen.

Meditate on: Philippians 2:1-30, Hebrews 12:12, 1 John 2:6

The Cleansing Agent – by Cynthia Quattrocelli

Then Jesus came to them and said, "All authority in Heaven and in earth has been given to me. Therefore, go and make disciples of all nations, baptizing them in the name of the Father and of the Son and of the Holy Spirit, and teaching them to obey everything I have commanded you. And surely, I am with you always, to the very end of the age."- Matthew 28:18-19

I tell you, whoever acknowledges me before men, the Son of Man will also acknowledge him before the angels of God. - Luke 12:8

Viewing the worn-looking Bible on the Janitor's work cart was a welcome sight for me in this nice Catholic hospital and nursing home. It is always a joyful occasion to find another devoted Christian at the work place. After a few weeks on the job, I met Rick, the Janitor. He was a sincere believer who carried the Word of God to read during his break times. A pleasant man and full of love for the residents, Rick always had a kind word for everyone.

Many of the older people there looked forward to the times when he would clean their rooms and the hallways where they lived. Rick knew each person's daily routine and he answered their requests for a helping hand. When serving them by doing easy errands they could not do themselves, he included conversations about God's love for them. Rick planted seeds of eternal hope in the hearts of his elderly friends. He gently directed them to put their faith in Jesus Christ. People called him, "Preacher Man."

On his free time, Rick visited with the residents and ministered to them from the Bible he kept on his cart. Next to his Bible sat the wash bucket filled with a cleaning solution. Remarkably, the One of whom Rick spoke to the people about -Jesus Christ, is *The Cleansing Agent* for our souls. If we confess our sins, He is faithful and just and will forgive us our sins and will *cleanse* us from all unrighteousness (1 John 1:9).

Our discussions together were uplifting about the goodness of God and how we desired all people in our path to know the reality of God in their lives. I was blessed to have had Rick, a brother, in my workplace. But you may be the only Christian where you work. Just remember; you and God are still a majority. When you stand out from the rest and live for the Lord and you know Almighty God is your Strength, you are not really the minority although it feels like you are. You have the same Power within you that raised Christ from the dead. God is on your side.

Ordained now, the "preacher man" has a church in a city community where he preaches God's Word encouraging the church to "Go" and make disciples of all people. He is zealous for the Lord!

Prayer: Dear Lord, help me as a Christian called by Your Name to obey the great commission when I go about my daily caregiving tasks. I do not want to be ashamed of the Gospel of Christ. By faith in You, I have a new life. Help me not forget to praise You and to thank You for all the benefits You paid for. By faith, You forgave all my sins and healed all my diseases. You – Lord, have crowned me with love and compassion, and You satisfy the desires of my heart with good things (Psalm 103:1-5). Thank You, Lord Jesus. Amen.

Meditate on: Daniel 12:3, John 21:15-17, Acts 10:42, Romans 1:16, Acts 1:8

And do not forget to do good

and to share

with others,

for with such sacrifices,

God is pleased.

Hebrews 13:16

"Tell Her She's Facing Eternity" - by Cynthia Quattrocelli

There are different kinds of gifts, but the same Spirit. There are different kinds of service, but the same Lord. There are different kinds of working, but the same God works all of them in all men. -1 Corinthians 12:4-6

Now to each one the manifestation of the Spirit is given for the common good. To one there is given through the Spirit the message of wisdom, to another the message of knowledge by means of the same Spirit. – 1 Corinthians 12:7-8

Cantankerous is the word I will use to describe the elderly woman who hired me to walk her dog and to clean her home. I felt uncomfortable around her. This was because of the way she verbalized her cleaning requests to me each time I arrived to work in her home. It was with harsh words and facial grimaces that she barked out her demands each time I went to clean there. There was a downright refusal on her part to engage in social conversation with me, but I prayed often for her.

She did once speak of how her son had been trying to get her to go to his church on Sundays. I said to her how I thought it was nice for him to offer to drive her to church each week. She only mumbled something negative about her daughter-in-law. She was convinced it was a "money" reason for her family to be coming around lately to visit. Although it was evident my client owned material wealth, I had a heavy heart for her. In my daily devotions, I prayed for her to know Christ.

The agreement we had was for me to come weekly and help her by cleaning two hours in whatever room needed attention. This included hands and knees cleaning and waxing her kitchen floor. Then the cellar stairs were to be swept and dry mopped.

One morning, as I was cleaning in the middle of her cellar stairs, the Holy Spirit suddenly spoke quite determinedly in my heart. He said, *"Tell her she's facing eternity."* I assure you this was not of my own thinking. I had only been engrossed in my cleaning. The intensity of this Word speaking within me, surprised me. Facing me now was the decision to obey or not to obey. At that point, I knew it was God and I had the impression that I was to do it right then.

This was an exceptional situation which required obedience. I had no fear, but Strength to follow through and to trust Him with the outcome. Immediately, I finished the last few steps and swiftly went to her with God's message on my lips. Unfortunately, after she heard what I said, she told me to get out and to not come back.

I often think about this woman and I hope she pondered this message from God and eventually found Christ as her Savior. I also hoped and prayed her son was given a "yes" to his invitation for her to go to his church to receive Christ's Love offer for eternal life.

In our daily lives, God may want us to speak to others in many ways. I wish my instruction from God to this client would have been a soft encouraging word. Unquestionably, God knew what needed to be said.

What would you have done if God asked you to do something like this? Would you have been willing? If you know God is asking you to do something, and you know for sure it is His request - seek to please Him. Jesus said, "I seek not to please Myself, but Him who sent Me" (John 5:30).

I may have lost a client, but because I obeyed God, I can have hope her soul was not lost. We know He has given to us the great commission - to be ambassadors for His Kingdom. How beautiful are the feet of those who proclaim Good News and proclaim salvation (Isaiah 52:7). My encounter with this elderly woman proved to me that keeping the people we help in our prayers is important to the Lord. He loves them so deeply.

Prayer: Father, I need to stay connected with You to do the work You have called me to do. Eagerly, I seek Godly Wisdom which is full of mercy bearing good fruit (James 3:17). As a caregiver, I will humble myself before You, my Mighty God and remember that I can do all things through Christ who strengthens me. At times, people may try to snuff out the Light of my lampstand, but my faith says that You will make a Way for them to hear the Good News again. Just as Joshua was strong and courageous, and the disciples preached without fear- help me to believe that You will go before me and accomplish through me fruit that will last. You will never leave me nor forsake me. In the Great Name of Jesus Christ, Amen.

Meditate on: Matthew 25:45, Luke 11:13, John 5:24, Romans 6:23, 1 Corinthians 12

Amazing Grace – by Cynthia Quattrocelli

For it is by grace you have been saved, through faith-and this not from yourselves, it is the gift of God - Ephesians 2:8

But when the kindness and love of God our Savior appeared, He saved us, not because of righteous things we had done, but because of His mercy, He saved us through the washing of rebirth and renewal by the Holy Spirit. - Titus 3:4-5

Singing to Clara was not something she or anyone had asked me to do, but I felt she needed the Best comfort I knew how to give her. She had been displaying signs of anxiety and was becoming a handful for the nursing staff. They were getting weary and running out of ideas at trying to protect her from falling out of bed. In her 90's, Clara did not understand how the UTI (urinary tract infection) attacking her body, was affecting her both physically and cognitively. What this elderly woman did grasp, is that she desperately wanted to get out of her room.

Before leaving Clara's room, the head Nurse respectfully said, "Clara, please lay back down on your bed." The Nursing staff's attempts proved unproductive. They called our Activities Department to see if we could generate a calming atmosphere for Clara. I sat in the chair beside the bed and held her hand. I began to sing *"Amazing Grace"* to her; she stared into my eyes. I truly did not know what to expect next. I was happy to note after a few stanzas of the hymn, that this once restless lady simply closed her eyes and went off to sleep.

Shyly, I walked passed the Nurse's desk on my way back to the Activities Department. I had been aware the door of the resident's room was wide open and the Nurse's desk was right outside her door. I like to sing, but I do not have a natural talent to sing. The hymn's words are God's love song to us. It will always sound good, whoever sings it. When there was no other answer to soothe this soul toward peace, I found the Best form of solace available - that being the life-giving *Amazing Grace* of our Lord Jesus Christ.

There was no way to be sure the outcome of this song was due to a faith in Christ for this elderly resident. She may have responded to the individual attention and she just fell asleep peacefully. My aim was to produce calmness. In addition, I believe the words in the hymn are anointed and may have been used by the Lord to plant faith in the heart of a Nurse.

I do know the Lord wants us to honor Him and to tell the Good News to all people. The Grace of God that brings salvation has appeared to all men (Titus 2:11). Even though most Americans are familiar with the hymn, *"Amazing Grace,"* there are many who have not connected to the true message it offers. As believers, let us be ready in faith to be a witness to those around us by stepping out of our comfort zone. He may not have you sing a hymn, but be watching and praying for Divine opportunities.

Prayer: Father, thank You. I am saved by grace and because of Christ, my sins are in the Sea of Forgetfulness. Help me to give the Gospel of God's Grace to others, so they too may have this same life-giving-love. I keep my communication open to You throughout each day as Your servant. Please help me to be aware of the answers You so willingly provide. Lord, You know all things and I desire more of You in my daily walk. Jesus, You are my Source of Strength when issues arise and I see no way out. Therefore, thank You ahead of time for the right direction, in everything I do for those I care for. In Christ's Beautiful Name, Amen.

Meditate on: Psalm 23, Proverbs 4:18, Romans 3:24,
2 Corinthians 113:14,
2 John 1:3

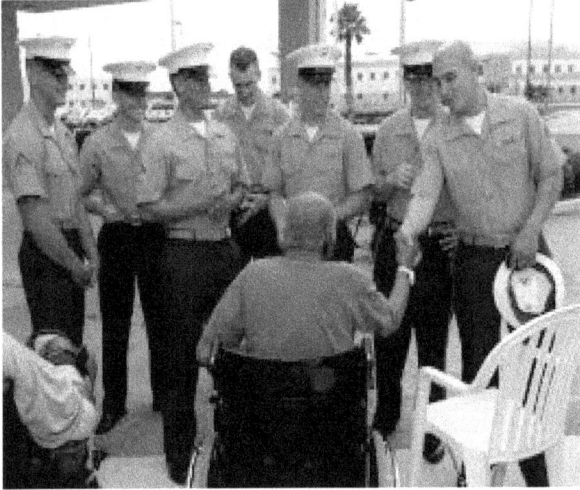

Rise in the presence of the aged,

show respect for the elderly

and

revere your God.

I am the Lord.

Leviticus 19:32

Come into My Heart – by Cynthia Quattrocelli

The Light shines in the darkness, but the darkness has not understood it. – John 1:5

To Him who loves us and has freed us from our sins by His Blood... -- Revelation 1:5

Marci was a mixture of different emotions depending on what was going on in her day. Although she was in her mid-sixties, Marci viewed the world by the little girl inside her. Because of her developmental disability of mild mental retardation, she reacted childishly when things were not going her way. Therefore, every day with Marci was unpredictable.

The staff at the nursing home where she lived knew her very well and they watched for outbursts of inappropriate behavior which often escalated, if not caught right off. Because of these instances, the staff grounded her. Everyone on the unit where she lived heard her temper tantrums and screaming when she struggled to get out of doing the simplest chores like taking a shower, making her bed, or cleaning up her room. The time-out discipline in her room was tough for Marci since she was a social being. She craved for attention. Staff felt that there was no reason, even in her sixties (mentally and emotionally she was about ten years old), that she could not learn to act more appropriately when challenged with a task.

For leisure time activities, I provided Marci with coloring books and simple puzzles. I presented her with sticker stars if she behaved and kept her room neat. But the best and most rewarding activity offered to her was when the Gospel Singers came to sing and to minister. Marci was a Born-Again Christian and I encouraged her to speak about her faith when we talked. Her Christian parents raised her and she came to live in this nursing home only after her Mom and Dad had passed on. When the Gospel Team came each month, she sang with delight (off-key to our ears, but I am sure it sounded lovely to the Creator's ears).

At the end of each program, Marci raised her hand to make a last request for them to sing, *"Come into My Heart, Lord Jesus"* (written by Harry D. Clarke). She then looked very content and proud that she had been the one to request the song which all of us were now singing. The song is so simple, but the message is clear: It invites people to call upon Jesus to live in their hearts.

Marci may have been a challenge for staff, but when the Spirit of God moved in those Gospel settings, she let her Light shine. Her faith in Christ shone bright to the personnel from every department as they poked their heads in to listen. Her face beamed with a sweet child-like faith. She was loving her Savior and singing an invitation for onlookers to ask Jesus to come into their hearts - to follow Him and not darkness and have the Light of Life. The love and peace of God unmistakably stood out in contrast to the usual gloom that consumes most nursing home environments.

We too can accelerate upon an opportunity to share the Light of the world - Jesus. One way to do this is to gain the trust of people over time and then share testimonies of our faith. We caregivers have a definite open door to help others understand how much God loves them. Step out in faith knowing this is just another part of giving care. Look around your daily environment and notice those who have not yet received the peace He offers. Eventually, show them the Way by inviting them to ask Jesus into their hearts. His arms are open-wide waiting to receive the lost, whoever they are, and whatever they have done.

Prayer: Heavenly Father, I praise You for who You are and who You say I am! Your Word says; I am the Righteousness of God by Christ Jesus. Please open hearts as I take opportunities to credit You with the hope I have… I no longer walk in darkness, I now have the Light of Life. I pray that those in my care will call upon the Name of Jesus. Help me guide people I see every day, showing them how to ask Jesus to come into their hearts. As Your child, I will keep my focus on You wherever I go. Lord, grow the Gospel seed I plant in co-workers, family, and visitors. I pray that they too will receive eternal life. Thanks, Holy Spirit for putting them on my heart. In Jesus Name, Amen.

Meditate on: Psalm 119:105, Matthew 18:4, John 1:9, 1 John 5-7, 2 Corinthians 4:6

Walking in Their Shoes – by Cynthia Quattrocelli

When you reap the harvest of your land, do not reap to the very edges of your field, or gather the gleanings of your harvest. Do not go over your vineyard a second time or pick up the grapes that have fallen. Leave them for the poor and the alien. I am the Lord your God. – Leviticus 19:9-10

Religion that God our Father accepts as pure and faultless is this: to look after orphans and widows in their distress and to keep oneself from being polluted by the world. – James 1:27

"Cindy, your goal is to gain an understanding of how a person feels when required to sit in a wheelchair trying to do activities of daily living with the use of only one arm," said the Professor. Back in 1990, this was the assignment given to me by my instructor as she taught her students to consider the physical limitations of a status-post CVA patient. Her attempt was to have each of the students in the Occupational Therapy Interventions class, to try *walking in their shoes.*

To do this project, I first decided on the age of the woman of whom I put myself in place of. I knew I wanted to help the elderly in my future job placement. I tried to recreate a typical scene in the bathroom imagining myself in her place. She must wash herself, brush her teeth, and fix her hair. All this had to be done, using only one hand.

Carrying out the assignment was a challenge. My sister who lived with me saw my attempts at trying to complete the tasks. There was no chance to cheat because Cathy was there and had to tell me to stop bringing my other hand out from behind my back even for a minute. It was amazing how much I relied on the second hand to aid me in everything I did. Over and over, I tried to open the small caps to the toothpaste and the make-up container only to drop them most times. At each episode, I had to reach down from my make-believe wheel chair to retrieve the tops.

Eventually, I got the hang of it. My fingers skillfully unscrewed the caps while stabilizing the object along my torso. This study was a necessary experiment for readying myself to help others. It put me in a position for *walking in their shoes*.

What came to my mind when completing this call to understand those in need of physical aid, is how God described the way He wanted a farmer to harvest his fields. By the farmer not reaping to the edges of his field or when he leaves the grapes on the ground for the poor, he gives food for the one who needs a helping hand in life (Leviticus 19:9-10). Caregivers, we have regard for the weak. By lending a supportive hand to those who have less ability to produce, we are in direct line with God's care for them. God displays His compassion through your actions each day.

Prayer: Dear Father in Heaven, The Lord Jesus walked through towns and villages feeding the multitudes and helping the poor and healing the sick. I am a caregiver who provides direct care and compassion for the people You love. Desiring to follow in His footsteps, I ask You for empathy, patience, guidance, wisdom, and understanding to help these I oversee. Help me by providing what I need to try and improve their quality of life. In Jesus Name, Amen.

Meditate: Psalm 41:1-3, Matthew 4:23-24, Ephesians 2:10, 2 Thessalonians 3:13

"God Help - Lord Help Me" - by Catherine Chambers

But the Helper, the Holy Spirit, whom the Father will send in My Name, will teach you all things and will remind you of everything I have said to you - John 14:26

Do not fear, for I am with you; do not be dismayed, for I am your God. I will strengthen you and help you; I will uphold you with my righteous right hand - Isaiah 41:10

Daily, the little lady in the Geri-chair yelled out the same word; "Help!" This seemed to be the only thing she knew how to say. She was legally blind and cognitively impaired as well. Obviously, it must have been difficult for her to understand that help was indeed close by. In desperation for her needs to be met, she constantly shouted her request throughout each day. When the nursing department had her up out of bed and seated in that special chair, it brought the most stress as her yelp could get annoying for staff and other residents. At meal times in the busy dining room, it became almost unbearable for staff to stay calm and collected and to hear the needs of others because all you could hear was her alarming loud cries for help.

One day as I was doing paperwork on the computer, she was right behind me. It seemed like every second I heard her loud ear-piercing screech; "help!" Even though the shrill cry made me want to run down the stairwells to escape, instead compassion arose within me. Approaching her slowly and with a gentle touch to her arm, I greeted her by name. I offered this hurting person to try something. My suggestion was to try saying, *"God help or Lord help me."* I continued by telling her how God hears your cry for help; He knows your needs.

The next words from her lips were "God help." Wow, I said to myself. Her response was a hope in me that she may have faith and be a Believer in the Lord Jesus. I then continued to assure her of His extravagant love and how He said, He will never leave her.

For the next one and a half years she lived there, the little lady with faith in her heart and a real need for her God, to come to her aid, exhibited peace. Yes, it is true - she still did call out, but it was to Him. It was a softer and a peaceful sounding plea, because she used the name, "Lord." He is indeed the Prince of Peace.

As Christian caregivers, I believe God directs us to be most concerned about the sensitivity of the person we care for. Their heart needs a loving God ministering to them in their troubles and bringing joy in their triumphs. If we focus on this part of our responsibilities, then some the inconveniences or irritations that we encounter will fade in comparison. In many ways, we care providers can guide and show a concern for the deep heart-cry of people. Your efforts directed by God Himself, can be specifically suited just for the person you aim to comfort.

Prayer: Praise be to the God and Father of our Lord Jesus Christ, the Father of compassion and the God of all comfort. I call upon You who comforts us in all our troubles. I know that You hear our cry for help. How blessed I am to have the Holy Spirit as my Helper. Lord, how grateful I am to know that You are an ever-present Help. I pray that by Your Holy Spirit, I will know what each person I am caring for needs. I pray they find Your peace. In Jesus' Name, Amen.

Meditate on: Psalm 54:4, Psalm 34:6, 2 Corinthians 1:3, 1 Peter 3:8

The righteous will flourish like a palm tree,

they will grow like a

cedar of Lebanon;

planted in the house of the Lord,

they will flourish in the courts of our God.

they will still bear fruit in old age,

they will stay fresh and green,

proclaiming, "The Lord is upright; He is my rock,

and there is no wickedness in Him."

Psalm 92:12-15

The Beautiful Word – by Catherine Chambers

For everything that is written in the past was written to teach us, so that through endurance and the encouragement of the scriptures, we might have hope. - Romans 15:4

All Scripture is God-breathed and is useful for teaching, rebuking, correcting, and training in righteousness. - 2 Timothy 3:16

The medical chart stated that Sandy had experienced abuse in her childhood. The devastations of the wrongdoings done to her, most likely led to her history of drug abuse. The impact of this lifestyle was evident.

Only in her 60's, this resident was young to be living in a nursing home. Daily, she would stroll aimlessly through the units in and out of other resident's rooms. With a flat expressionless face and what appeared to us as scary-looking eyes, she kept her gaze straight ahead. Sandy did not focus on anyone or anything. When approached by staff, she gave no response. Her countenance came across as being - "out there."

My co-worker, Terese and I wanted to visit with Sandy to read God's Word to her especially when we noted recently she was not walking the floors as much. In times spent with Sandy, we recognized for entire days she had taken to just laying on her bed with eyes closed. The Nursing staff reported; "this resident is refusing to eat." It appeared, she was giving up on life. We asked each other; what should we do?

As Spiritual leaders in the nursing home, we first prayed together in the facility's Chapel before going to see her. I felt the strong Power of God's love and His Wonderful Peace. His Presence was with us at our visits. Both of us ministered to her and told her about God's love for her. We gave her the Gospel, told her our testimonies of His goodness in our lives, and prayed the Lord's Prayer. One day, I read Psalm 34 telling her the Lord is close to the brokenhearted. At the close of each visit, we came together and prayed for Sandy before leaving the room.

In all the times, spent sitting at her bedside proclaiming God's Word and His Goodness through Christ, we never saw any physical sign or verbal confirmation that she understood or received anything we said. But our faith never swayed. We know God's Word does not return to Him void. In Isaiah 55:11, God says, "My Word that goes out from My mouth will not return to Me empty, but will accomplish what I desire and achieve the purpose for which I sent It." We relied on *the Beautiful Word of God.*

Terese and I had visited Sandy daily for the last two weeks of her life. On those occasions, we never stopped believing while continuing to pray that our Faithful Lord and Savior would make Himself known to her.

Where is your faith at? Do you struggle with circumstances at the job or even in your own family that bring a sense of hopelessness? Let me encourage you to give it over to the Lord...cast your cares upon Him for He tenderly cares for you. Pray unceasingly.

Now faith is being sure of what we hope for and certain of what we do not see (Hebrews 11:1). Jesus said, whatever you ask for in prayer, believe that you have already received it, and it will yours (Mark 11:24). Therefore, try speaking into existence what you are believing for. Then thank Him for the answer. Faith moves mountains.

Continue to believe even if the answer does not come right away. Reviewing who God is helps me in the times of waiting and wondering when, how, and why. Righteousness and Justice are the foundation of His throne; Love and Faithfulness go before Him (Psalm 89:14). Meditate on each one of those words - speaking them aloud. If you embrace HIS attributes each time you get off the HOPE track, you will find that there is no answer, but to TRUST HIM. He said, "Be still and know that I am God." (Psalm 46:10)

Prayer: Dear Lord Jesus, I am grateful for the truth of Your Living Word. I am empowered with the promised Holy Spirit to help me in the responsibilities I perform on earth. Teach me to take Your Words literally. You said to speak to the mountains in our lives without doubting...believing we have already received what we have asked for. Therefore, I will learn to look at my circumstances and declare with faith what I believe Your Word says should happen. Help me to know You have heard my prayers. Even when answers do not come my way, because You are God, I will rest in You. In Jesus Name, Amen.

Meditate on: Proverbs 3:5, Matthew 4:1-25, Romans 8:26-27, Hebrews 4:12-16

A "God Assignment" – by Cynthia Quattrocelli

And do not forget to do good and to share with others, for with such sacrifices, God is pleased. – Hebrews 13:16

"Give to the one who asks you, and do not turn away from the one who wants to borrow from you. – Matthew 5:42

I got a call for help from a friend one day while at my job as an in-home Senior Companion Aide. This friend who also was my Bible study teacher was asking if I would have the time to sit once week with a neighbor of hers. This widowed neighbor was in her late 70's and she was a Believer. Bernice had been expressing extreme fear lately to the point of saying she knew there was a man in her attic. My friend explained to me that where Bernice lived, there was no attic. Bernice lived in a one floor senior apartment building. The only "attic" was an upper crawl space allowing for repair to the heating or air-conditioning units.

A couple of days later, we went together to visit Bernice. She was a slender attractive woman. She was wearing make-up and had a cute stylish haircut. You could not miss the sweet Southern twang in her speech. After being there for only a short while, it was clear this darling widow liked to do most of the talking. On the wall, in her living room, hung a large painting of Christ. She spoke briefly about how she loved Him, but in the same breath told me about the "strange things" going on in her home at, this Senior-Living apartment complex. I was introduced as a new friend who will begin to visit her once a week to do her shopping and light cleaning. Bernice was happy to hear this and mentioned how her children forgot about her, as she put it.

Before and after weekly shopping trips, Bernice filled me in on the "goings-on" with the neighbors there. She showed me her proof of how a certain man living nearby had been in her apartment and messed with her belongings. One piece of her evidence was her tangled up jewelry. She believed that someone came and did this. Then she began to tell me about the noises in the crawl space above the kitchen. She described sleepless nights of fretting and worrying. "Going to sleep in my bedroom is out of the picture," Bernice said, while she pointed to her new "bed," the couch. I thoughtfully summed it up; these stories were all fictitious and created out of fear. Her mind was deceiving her and I knew the source of it. Yes, the enemy of the soul. But, I thought to myself, she is a Christian and simply needs more Truth of God's Word to help her find His peace.

Each time I visited, I listened with patience to Bernice' testimonies about how people were out to get her. When I did have a few chances to jump in to the conversations, I tried to quote comforting scripture. I hoped she may remember the verses and use them toward this battle waging in her mind. I felt if I could help her stay focused on the One who is her Strength, then she could live in her home, without dread. On one occasion, I brought a CD with me. It was praise music. I was hoping it would help her.

Eventually, as time went on she began to devise ways to be free from living in this place. A move to a safer location was all she spoke of. Her children did not want to talk with her on the phone and never visited. She said, they thought she was crazy when she would express the horror she felt living there. So, they never called her. Bernice had no one.

After my attempts of praying with her and giving her some solid Spiritual nuggets from God's Word, to fight against these attacks of fear, I saw how she was not getting it. Considering how the Lord loves her and taking my responsibility to obey Him by helping a lonely widow, I began to have understanding and direction. I needed to get practical help for her.

It certainly would have been possible for her to walk in Christ's authority which brings Believers the freedom He paid for. She could have experienced life to the full without fear (John 10:10). If she had understood it was necessary to work at building up her faith with the ammunition I brought to her, (the sword of the Spirit which is the Word of God), then her faith could have released her from this bondage of fear. Apostle Paul tells us to be strong in the Lord and in His mighty power. Ephesians 6 gives us the assignment to equip ourselves with the armor of God. We are to stand our ground and find peace through the troubles our Lord warned us about. Jesus taught us by saying, "In this world, you will have trouble. But take heart! I have overcome the world" (John 16:33). He gave us the keys to the Kingdom. Christ paid for our victory.

I found out the name of Bernice's doctor and called him. I filled him in on her unbelievable stories - true only to Bernice. Others may have thought of her as a little "off the wall." I told him on a voicemail message about the bizarre things she said were happening to her at this apartment and how she threatened to walk along the highway to get to a friend's house in another town. I gave my name and explained my relationship with Bernice and my deep concern for my new friend. I had grown fond of her and she said I was her Angel.

She often called me at home and I felt blessed when she said that hearing my voice soothed her. This was especially true for her when she called at dusk. Her fear heightened that time of day. I reassured her. I said how she had a nice safe home there and God loves her and He was with her. I knew in my heart; this person should not be living on her own. I sought the Lord diligently for an answer.

Months past and I had not heard back from the doctor. One day I mentioned to Bernice how I had once worked as a Companion Aide at the local assisted living facility, less than a mile from her. She knew about this place. Now a new scheme started in her head to get out of her "dangerous" home. She said," I want to live there." Later that week, I decided to treat her to coffee and a pastry at a local spot and then offered to drive her over to the facility. It was indeed a long shot, because to live in a place like this is expensive and her only resources came from her deceased husband's social security benefits.

Bernice was greeted kindly at the facility and they offered to have us stay for lunch. We did and enjoyed it. She made friends quickly with the receptionist there. This caring woman told Bernice they offer respite care which are short-term stays in the facility.

I called the administrator and informed her of Bernice's situation. I wanted this person in charge to understand how the children of this widow woman were not helping her and seemed to have excommunicated themselves from her.

Bernice was so happy to tell me of her stay in the facility the next time we talked. After that, my dear friend was more adamant than ever to move there. She had felt safe with so many staff people to care for her. For some reason, we kind of lost communication for a month or so. One day, I went out to her apartment to visit after getting no response to my phone call.

I felt in my heart she must have indeed moved when no one answered at her door. I got back in the car and drove over to the Senior Home and I was elated to find out she was now a permanent resident there. Praise the Lord! God is very Faithful to His children.

A couple of times, I took the other woman I was caring for along with me to visit Bernice in her safe new abode. We all enjoyed a nice lunch with her. Bernice said the people in charge told her they liked her and that is why this was her home now. As I look back on it all, I know it was a *God Assignment* for me. God used me and my past affiliations at the assisted living home to get her out of a place that caused her to lose sleep. Her situation could have ultimately brought more harm to her health. He knew I would be willing to help by driving her to this senior home of which she had only heard about. Bernice probably would have been unable to convince them to take her in without my input. She needed a trusted spokesperson.

I am not sure how this living arrangement is paid for. Perhaps her kind Doctor pays the balance of the monthly bill. It just may be, the facility just could not put this Southern sweetheart out. Whatever reason, compassion took over.

Is God calling you to help someone in a tangible way. Is there someone in your life who has no one to speak for them? Do you know someone who needs a ride? Does one of your neighbors need a visit from time to time? Reach out as the Lord leads you - praying for His direction. Speak up for those who cannot speak for themselves (Proverbs 31:8).

Prayer: Heavenly Father, You are the God of compassion - the God of all comfort, who comforts us in all our troubles, so that we can comfort those in any troubles with the same comfort we ourselves have received from You (2 Corinthians 1:3-4). I know You are the One who is the Defender of widow. I praise You and I rejoice in knowing that You are the One who sets the lonely in families. Hallelujah! Continue the good work You have started in me, as a caregiver. Put a desire in my heart to be an example of Your love to those around me. Help me to be aware of God Assignments and to remember to invite the Holy Spirit to empower me - because apart from You, I can do nothing. In Jesus Name, amen.

Meditate on: Psalm 68:5-6, Proverbs 15:25, John 14:14, John 15:5, Philippians 2:1-4, 1 Timothy 5:5, James 1:27,

Two Ten Dollar Bills – by Cynthia Quattrocelli

If anyone does not provide for his relatives, and especially for his immediate family, he has denied the faith and is worse than an unbeliever. - 1 Timothy 5:8

Remember this; Whoever sows sparingly will reap sparingly, and whoever sows generously will also reap generously. - 2 Corinthians 9:6

"Those *two ten-dollar bills* with the one-dollar bill in my pocket was to me like having $201.00", Bud exclaimed. Coming from a poor family, this event appeared to be a powerful and momentous time in our neighbor's life. He is now 94 years old. Bud was sharing this and other stories with us recently about the days of his youth. He was describing the moment he had received his very first pay from the Army back in the early 1940's, at the age of 17. He went on to explain how he had promptly sent home his pay of *two ten-dollar bills* to his Momma in West Virginia and kept the one-dollar bill to buy some shaving equipment. Grinning, he reminisced how prices were lower back then. He added how he had planned to buy a comb and several other essentials with the dollar he would keep on the next pay day. In detail, Bud shared with us his plan at the time to send his Momma the twenty dollars from each pay. With a twinkle in his eye, Bud reminisced, "the Army supplied all my meals, so I just kept sending Momma the $20 each pay-day." He followed this pattern for the next four or more years he had served in the Army.

Upon arriving home after his time of duty, Bud's Mother presented him with a jar from her kitchen cabinet. It surprised him to find it filled with all his ten-dollar bills. Added up, it came to around $10,000. His Mom had saved all his money and any extra he sent home while he was away. A brief time later, his mother who had been having trouble walking, explained to him how the house they had been living in since his boyhood was becoming more difficult to get to from the road. That home was located on a very high hill. Her son wanted to help her to find a different home. They knew of one closer to the road. When inquiring about the price, Bud had a confirmation of this being the right one after finding out the house cost $10,000; just the amount he had in the jar.

Bud continued his life story telling us how eventually, he married and became the main caregiver to his wife for most of their marriage. She had suffered with a chronic illness and had been dependent upon him to help her with everything. He held a fulltime job, but when coming home he had the job of cooking, cleaning, and caring for their child too. Years past, and Bud became a widower.

We met him when he was in his late eighties and my husband and I moved into the house next door to him. He has always invited us to pick the blueberries from his front yard bush and every summer has delivered fresh home-grown tomatoes from his garden, right to our door. A blessing came to our friendly neighbor at age 86. He met and married a beautiful Christian lady who was in her late 70's. You know what they say; It's never too late!

Recently, my husband injured his leg and was out of work for several months. Our good neighbor Bud, came over to check on us, because for several weeks, he saw my husband's van parked in the driveway during regular work hours. After we informed him of the details of the injury and the Doctor's prognosis, Bud came back the next day and handed us a $100.00 bill. He blessed us and we thanked him. Again, two weeks later, he gave my husband another hundred dollars. We tried to tell him he did not have to do that, but looking at my husband, he said, "after all, you're not working." Now it is our turn to pour blessings out to Bud and his wife. She has been having trouble walking lately, so we are planning to fix a nice Sunday dinner to take over to their house and spend time with them in Christian fellowship.

I have taken notice that if we meditate on and apply God's Word and observe with God's Grace the lives of those around us, we will clearly see the Holy Spirit directing us. Be sensitive to the leading of God who lives in your heart. He loves all those you meet on your daily path. Listen to Him. He is always speaking. Our obedience brings praise and honor to God from the lives we help. Bud had honored his Mother and God blessed him (Exodus 20:12). He loved his wife just as Christ loved the church when he cared for her daily needs (Ephesians 5:28-29). He took opportunity to do good to us by loving us (his neighbor) as himself when he gave grocery money two times when my husband could not work (Matthew 22:39). This friend of ours has always shone the Light of Christ through his actions.

We are thankful for the Christian upbringing and the example his mother provided to him. By her doing what the Bible taught regarding training up your children, this dear Christian Mother's influence reached us and many others who have been touched by her son's kind helpfulness. The Divine domino effect from his ancestor's choice to live according to God's Word still cascades onto the path he takes.

Prayer: Dear Father God, as a caregiver, I want to be sensitive to the work of the Holy Spirit in me and in others. Show me the areas in my life needing more of Your Word applied for producing right actions toward others. If I am not spending regular "alone" time with You to take in my daily bread from the scriptures, help me get back to that special place with You. Lord, would you guide me to a Christian radio or T.V. station to aid me in learning the Word, therefore helping to renew my mind to the things of God. The outcome may be significant one day to another and all because of the redirection of my steps. Lord, help me to aim at declaring; "more of You and less of me." In Jesus Name, amen.

Meditate on: Psalm 145:4, Proverbs 22:9, Proverbs 19:17,

2 Corinthians 9:12,

1 John 3:17

They will Still Bear Fruit in Old Age
- by Cynthia Quattrocelli

You did not choose me, but I chose you and appointed you to go and bear fruit-fruit that will last. – John 15:16

Put on the full armor of God so that you can take your stand against the devil's schemes. – Ephesians 6: 11

I am now realizing, as years have passed since her death, Rosie was more of a mentor to me than I had understood then. For years I drove her to church each week. We first met at a Christian single women's meeting, but it was not until a few years later we both discovered we could be a help to one another. She was 90 years old, a widow, and needed a ride to church every Sunday. I was looking for a new church since I had recently moved too far from where I had been going. One day, I visited her to see how she was doing in the assisted living facility she had recently moved to. She mentioned a church she had seen close by to her new home. A plan started to unfold; I would start picking her up each week and we would go to church together.

I believe we both noticed the Hand of God in all this. It blessed her to be able to go out to worship each week; to happily express her sweet love for Christ. I liked having a companion because it is always nice when you go to a new church to have someone to sit with. It is tough to be single and sit alone in church. I love Seniors too. We got along very well.

Being responsible to drive someone to church can also help get one self to church each week without excuse. In addition, we both needed the friendship. It was a perfect arrangement.

Every week after church, I drove her to the nearest Tim Horton's Coffee Shop. We enjoyed talking and eating lunch together. It was Rosie who listened to my prayers about wanting to be married someday and it was she who comforted me when I cried about being lonely. She told me that God is hearing your prayers and He is working out all the details to bring you the right man while He develops your walk with Him. I recall her telling me to just trust Him.

She had struggles too. They were clashes with some of the folks who lived at the same Senior Home. She was not accustomed to the idea of having so many neighbors living very close to her and sharing meals together. Until recently, Rosie had been quite independent as a widow. She had stayed in her own home up to age 90. Amazingly, even in her nineties, God was continuing to develop her. She felt tested as disagreements with certain fellow tenants nudged her to hold her tongue and to pray for those who verbally mistreated her (Matthew 5:44). Although, like any of us, at other times she messed up and did not keep her peace.

In some of the conflicts, she had a right to speak up and speak up she did. I listened to her explain to me her attempts at offering an important suggestion to the management there. She asked staff for permission to schedule an added monthly visiting church. The church that was already visiting regularly was very religious and did not offer the Gospel message. They gave communion for all in attendance without even giving an invitation for them to call upon Christ as their as Savior.

She was out-numbered with her request; no one else voted to have another church minister there. Listening to her experiences, I gave her the same patience she had displayed to me when I had shared my personal burdens with her. I consoled her when she spoke about how the same ladies were always cruel to her because she lifted up the Name of Jesus in prayer before meals. Rosie knew that God still wanted to use her in her old age; she had a burden for the souls there who did not know the Lord Jesus as Savior.

God declares in Psalm 92:12 & 14; "The righteous will flourish like a Palm tree; *They will still bear fruit in old age.*" This woman after God's own heart learned to rise above the insults and criticisms and chose instead to give a gentle answer to those who were in opposition to her (Proverbs 15:1). It did not mean that she gave up on praying and trying to encourage the staff to arrange monthly visits from a Gospel-based Church to come and minister to her neighbors. Rosie had a calling on her life to be an ambassador for Christ at this new dwelling.

During our Sunday friendship outings, she often guided me with the following statement: "Remember this every morning; ask the Lord to put a guard over your mind." This caring and direct advice reminded me how Apostle Paul instructed us in Ephesians 6:10-18; to "Stand your ground and put on the full armor of God...."

I still recall my good friend's words and I am even more aware how she prepared me to be strong for success in battle against the rulers of this dark world. It is not flesh and blood (our neighbors, families, anyone, etc.) that we are up against, but it's the spiritual forces of evil in the heavenly realms we do battle with (2 Corinthians 10:3-6). Take your stand against opposition as you put on the full armor of God to bear fruit for the Kingdom of God. Take up the sword of the Spirit which is the Word of God. As you offer prayer for another, go to God's Word and where there is a pronoun, put the names of those you are praying for in that spot. This is faith.

Looking back, I now view Rosie as a pillar of Faith. Though short in stature, she was a strong woman of God fighting against the evil forces who were trying to stop the Gospel from going forth. I do not know if her desire to have that Christ-centered church scheduled at the Home ever did materialize. What I do know is this: she was a loving Christian influence for many young staff people there. I heard reports about her praying over some who had an open heart to know Jesus. She testified concerning a few of them coming to have faith. And God only knows the Divine outcome that her stance for Christ preached, had influenced her neighbors.

Prayer: Dear Heavenly Father, thank You for the beautiful friends and mentors You place in my life. Help me to recognize just how important they are to me. Help me Lord, to notice that because of their influence; I am learning so much and my faith is being developed. I want to be teachable at any age. I too want to bear fruit for the Kingdom of God in my old age. Lord, every morning, put a guard over my mind. Holy Spirit, help me see the thoughts I should take captive to the obedience of Christ. Keep us safe from the evil one and deliver us from the fowler's snare (Psalm 91:3). For You have called us to bear fruit that will last (John 15:16). Hallelujah! In Jesus Name, Amen.

Meditate on: Psalm 71:9-18, Proverbs 20:29, 2 Corinthians 10:4-5, 2 Timothy 1:7, Philippians 3:20-21

"How Do You Get to Heaven?" – by Cynthia Quattrocelli

For it is by grace that you have been saved, through faith-and this not from yourselves, it is a gift of God- not by works, so that no one can boast. -Ephesians 2:8-9

"Believe in the Lord Jesus, and you will be saved- you and your household."
-Acts 16:31

Joyfully, leading as a Dementia-Care Activities Leader, many times I incorporated Spiritual-based activities into the cognitive or social programs. Sitting around that colossal wooden table each day doing a variety of hands-on activities were four to five ladies in the age range of 80-95 years old. They were certainly a light-hearted group. My goal was to have them become a functioning participant in activity programs daily.

When I directed this bunch toward Spiritual things, I was sensitive to their past church affiliations. We took turns reading the large-print scripture verses I had printed out for them. We enjoyed Hymn sing-a-longs, prayed together, and I even provided Rosary beads to those who were familiar with this way of praying.

Although many times, while we took part in these activities of Faith, I wondered if my dear residents around the table knew for sure if they would go to Heaven someday. Because I cared about them, I wanted to hear it in their own words. My purpose was to open-up an opportunity for them to find Christ if they really did not know the Lord as Savior.

I took turns by going around the table addressing each one by name and asking; "What do you think - how do you get to Heaven?" Most there, expressed their hope in Jesus Christ for going to Heaven when they died. This pleasantly surprised me.

The first thing out of their mouths was, "Jesus died on the cross to take away our sins." For the ones that sat silent, I had them or another resident read aloud John 3:16. I then asked if they believed in Jesus Christ. I followed it up by asking if they wanted prayer.

When you are in the position of caregiver for anyone, but especially for the elderly or for those with chronic illnesses, I believe God would have us use respect for the individual while offering them the free-gift of salvation. I liked the idea of presenting this personal question to my residents and letting them speak for themselves. Most times, in the life of a person with dementia, others tend to do the thinking and speaking for them. Time and time again, I have experienced remarkable responses from those in my care when they're given the chance to speak on their own.

On the other hand, it is true there may be circumstances where this open opportunity for them to speak is not applicable. This is the case for the person who is physically incapable of verbalizing. If someone is just defiant, we can pray for their hearts to be open by asking the Holy Spirit how we can convey the Gospel of God's love to them. They too, may unlock their heart to hearing about how the Lord loves them by you performing daily caregiving tasks using kind, considerate, and consistent, methods mixed with carefully thought-out words aimed at showing them the Way, the Truth, and the Life. Gain their trust. Our determination should be to make our gentleness be known to all. The Lord is near.

Prayer: Heavenly Father, my prayer is for the one who is in my care who does not know the promise of eternal life through Your Son, Jesus Christ. Your Word says do not be anxious about anything, but by prayer and petition, with thanksgiving, present your requests to God. I ask You to open their heart to the Gospel of Christ and to use my care methods and words to minister Your love to them. In Jesus Name, amen.

Meditate on: John 3:3-5, John 6:38-40, Acts 2:38, Romans 3:23, Colossians 4:2-6

Activity Ideas for People with Dementia

Spiritual Ideas:

-Sing-a-longs with familiar hymns can awaken Christian roots in an individual. At these gatherings, the Holy Spirit can move in hearts. The caregiver then has an opportunity to offer prayer and showing God's love for them.

-Attendance to church services

-Displaying traditional religious symbols

-Reading or listening to Bible scriptures

-Reciting common prayers

-Taking the hand of the person to pray specifically for them

-Ask a small group of people to take turns speaking out things they are thankful to God for. Write the list on a large board for all to see and then have open discussion. Simple Bible trivia is fun too.

These ideas have brought remarkable results to inspire individuals with a low-functioning cognitive level to reminisce favorably about their faith.

"Call on Jesus" – by Cynthia Quattrocelli

For, everyone who calls upon the name of the Lord will be saved. – Romans 10:13

Just as a man is destined to die once, and after that to face judgment, so Christ was sacrificed once to take away the sins of many people; and He will appear a second time, not to bear sin, but to bring salvation to those who are waiting for Him. - Hebrews 9:27-28

This resident was new to my assigned unit at the nursing home and he was younger than the average patient there. He was probably in his thirties. Of course, we are not allowed to know the details of why such an unlikely person would need to live in a skilled nursing facility, but I was curious.

We said our usual introductions the first time I visited him. I informed him of how our Activity Department can provide movies, books, magazines, or music with a radio or CD's for him. Turning to leave, I called back to him saying, "just let a nurse know and they can summons me to bring the items to your room." I had left in haste because I could see this was going to be a challenging case. I sensed a hard wall around him. I recognized he was not going to be receptive to any offers of kindness. He may have displayed this unfriendliness because of the harsh reality of his situation.

I planned to take a bold approach next time by testing him to see if he would bring up any faith. I was hoping faith existed, although, I detected a spirit of atheism. I made a point to go and say hello to him each time I was near the unit where he was. He shared a room with a resident who was out all day, so I had freedom to talk with him openly.

Always praying first for this young man moments before visiting him, God lead me to tell him about Jesus reciting John 3:16. I then clearly announced the Romans 10:13 verse - "For, everyone who calls upon the name of the Lord, will be saved." Every time I went to see him, my heart was determined to help him discover how very simple it was to find God; I would sweetly say, *"Call on Jesus."* With love for the patient and honor to the Lord, I have always tried to go and proclaim the goodness of God and His plan of salvation to everyone in my care. I try to open their hearts to His love by saying to them, "God loves you; look how wonderfully He made you."

I was only given a few short weeks at attempting to make clear the love of God to this man. The Holy Spirit had been giving me a heads-up by showing me he did not have much time to live. He died within weeks of moving there. My heart cried to God saying, he died too young. The last time I saw him, I had made an extreme effort toward his conversion when I repeated my direction of, *"Call on Jesus."* He looked right at me and spoke it back to me in a mocking-tone. I tried again by saying, "All I can tell you is, when the time comes, call on Jesus!" I then said, "God Bless you," and I left the room.

God only knows what happened after that. We need to do our part to carry the Good News to the lost, and then find rest in the fact that we did obey the Lord, by lovingly sharing what was revealed to us. Our hope and faith can be for folks like this to have the Lord appear to them in the last moment of life. We do not know if then - they may have the chance to repent and be saved. God tells us who exalt Him, to be still and know that He is God (Psalm 46:10). We do the witnessing; God waters; God saves.

Prayer: Dear Father, I praise You and thank You for every day. Thank You for the Word You planted within me. Help me to proclaim it boldly to those in my care. In Psalm 41:1-3, You tell me that blessed is the man/woman who has regard for the weak; and the Lord delivers him in times of trouble. I trust in You and continue to look to You for opportunities for giving my testimony. You opened my heart to hear the plan of salvation. Thank You for opening the heart of _____, whom I am a caring for. I pray they will have faith in Christ. In Jesus Name, Amen.

Meditate on: Psalm 41:16, Romans 4:25, Romans 8:5-8, Hebrews 9:27, Jude 1:17-18.

The Presence of the Holy Spirt - by Catherine Chambers

And let us consider how we can spur one another on toward love and goods deeds. Let us not give up meeting together, as some are in the habit of doing, but let us encourage one another-and all the more as you see the Day approaching. – Hebrews 10:24-25

If you have any encouragement from being united with Christ, if any comfort from His love, if any tenderness and compassion, then make my joy complete by being like-minded, having the same love, being one in spirit and purpose. -Philippians 2:1-2

People were flooding into the dining room used for church services. While busy helping the residents, who needed direction on where to sit, I took a glance around the room and saw Todd at the doorway. His wife was pushing his wheelchair. Nothing unusual for Todd's attendance at this and all church meetings; it was the expression on his face that moved my heart.

My friend Todd, is a sweet Christian man. Even though his speech sounds muffled due to a stroke, he is accustomed to making blunt yet kind and directive comments. This day, I saw him crying with much emotion. I went over to him and it was obvious the Presence of the Holy Spirit brought him to tears. The CD player used each week was for playing praise and worship music while the congregants made their way into the service. But this day, the worship ushered in a rich manifestation of the Holy Spirit bringing Divine comfort in many hearts.

Knowing that God's Presence was there and while weeping, he lovingly inquired if myself and another worker, Terese, were Spirit-filled Christians. He already knew we were professing Christians, but he took direction from the Counselor Himself, the sweet Holy Spirit, to ask us if we were baptized in the Holy Spirit. He shared with us and with others later, about receiving the infilling or the baptism in the Holy Ghost (Acts 1:4-5).

I agree with Todd to help the church be aware of and ask for, an increased evidence of the Holy Spirit. He comes to live in you upon salvation, but have you asked for the baptism in the Holy Spirit? He is the promise from God that Jesus commanded the disciples to wait for in Acts 1:4. I believe we should discover and receive all the Lord has for us. We have a better Covenant. It includes the Power from the Holy Spirit. Apostle Paul did not want the brethren to be ignorant; read how he describes the Holy Spirit and Spiritual gifts in 1 Corinthians chapters 12-15.

Some churches offer a Spiritual gifts test. I have taken this test. The results can help you to discover interests or leadings you have always noticed in your life. The Lord wants to empower these gifts by baptizing you in the Holy Spirit. His Power will enable you to serve the Lord more fully and effectively (Acts 1:8).

Follow the way of love and eagerly desire spiritual gifts, especially the gift of prophecy. Everyone who prophesies speaks to men for their strengthening, encouragement, and comfort (1Corinthians 14:1-3).

Prayer: Heavenly Father, thank You for sending us another Helper - the Holy Spirit. He is our Strength, our Comforter, our Counselor, etc. I seek to know Him better and I pray for the baptism in the Holy Spirit. Lord, I am going to study Your Word and follow through with the leading You provide concerning this One who was spoken about by the Prophet Joel: "In the last days, God says, I will pour out My Spirit on all people. Your sons and your daughters will prophecy…" (Joel 2:28-32 and Acts 2:16-21)

Meditate on: Isaiah 11:2, Matthew 3:11, Romans 8:26, Acts 1:8,

Acts 2:38, Ephesians 5:18

And You Will Be My Witnesses – by Catherine Chambers

Today, if you hear His voice, do not harden your hearts. -Hebrews 4:7

The harvest is plentiful, but the workers are few. Ask the Lord of the harvest, therefore, to send out workers into his harvest field. -Luke 10:2

Those who look to the Lord are radiant! This describes Star, an RN on staff at the nursing home where I work. Together with her usual nursing duties, this minister of God's love finds time to refill Elma's wheelchair tote with hard candy, carefully listens with a heart of gold as she daily applies make-up to the ripened faces of the elderly women there, and frequently offers a smile and word of encouragement to me, as her sister in the Lord.

When I step back and attempt to look at this environment through God's eyes, I see the workers He has placed here to minister and bring in the harvest. Gail, a cleaning woman at my work place, has been a source of encouragement to me since day one. She is open with her faith and we have times of sharing in what we see God doing here. Recently, I was ministering in my role as Spiritual Care Leader to a resident who was very sick. Upon leaving his bedside and entering the hallway, Gail approached me and said, "I heard you talking to that resident and you gave him the whole gospel, you said it all to him."

Gail's statement helped reassure me; it brought a reminder of how God specifically called me to "visit the lonely." Each one of us has been called to "go" and minister to those who the Lord has placed in our lives. Some will plant, some will water, but only God makes things grow (1 Corinthians 3:6-9). Recently, I heard someone say about the Lord, "He is the Good News God!" People need to know how much God loves them. God wants them to know He has prepared an eternal home for them. Jesus proved the validity of His testimony by saying, "I have not come on my own; but He sent Me" (John 8:42). Are you ready to "go" and proclaim the Good News to the sick, the lonely, and the lost? God sent Jesus – and Jesus sent you.

Allow your love-walk with Jesus to be who you are always. He wants to take preeminence in all you do.

Prayer: Dear Father in Heaven, As I go and proclaim the Good News to the lost, my Strength is from the Lord. I am not ashamed of the gospel of Christ. God of Peace, equip me with everything good, for doing Your will. May You work in me what is pleasing to You, through Jesus Christ. To Him be the glory for ever and ever. I seek to follow the way of love and fan into flame the gift of God which is in me, through the laying on of hands. In Jesus Name, Amen.

Meditate on: Psalm 34:5, Psalm 49:15, Isaiah 61:1-3,
2 Corinthians 3:12,
Titus 2:7-8

Conclusion:

Caregivers

are in line with

God's character.

Regardless of your title,

the role of caregiving is close to the

heart of God – He is the ultimate Caregiver!

The Beatitudes define our role.

Each line can speak to God-focused caregivers.

The verses start with,

blessed are those who....and they end with

the eternal promise of nearness to God.

(Matthew 5:1-12)

Can you see yourself here?

Index: Caregiving Bible Verses

God's Words to pray for those who are <u>sick</u>:

Psalm 91:2-3 - I will say of the Lord, "He is my refuge and my fortress, my God, in whom I trust." Surely, He will save me from the fowler's snare and from deadly pestilence.

Isaiah 53:4-5 - Surely, He took up our infirmities and carried our sorrows, yet we considered Him stricken by God, smitten by Him, and afflicted. But He was pierced for our transgressions, He was crushed for our infirmities; the punishment that brought us peace was upon Him, and by His wounds, we are healed.

Jeremiah 32:27 – "I am the Lord, the God of all mankind. Is anything too hard for me?"

Matthew 4:4 - Jesus answered, "It is written: man does not live by bread alone, but by every word that comes from the mouth of God".

Matthew 6:6 - But when you pray, go into your room, close the door, and pray to your Father, who is unseen.

Matthew 8:13 - Then Jesus said the centurion, "Go! It will be done just as you believed it would." And his servant was healed that very hour.

Matthew 9:22 – "Take heart, daughter," He said, "your faith has healed you". And the woman was healed from that moment.

Matthew 18:19-20 – "Again, I tell you that if two of you on earth agree about anything you ask for, it will be done for you by My Father in Heaven". For where two or three come together in My name, there I am with them".

Mark 1:41-42 – Filled with compassion, Jesus reached out His hand and touched the man, "I am willing, "He said, "Be clean." Immediately, the leprosy left him and he was cured.

Mark 9:23 – "Everything is possible for him who believes".

Mark 11:22 – "Have faith in God."

Mark 11:24 – "Therefore, I tell you, whatever you ask for in prayer, believe that you have received it, and it will be yours".

Mark 11:25 – "And when you stand praying, if you hold anything against anyone, forgive him, so that your Father in Heaven may forgive you your sins".

Index: Caregiving Bible Verses

God's Words to pray for those who are <u>sick</u>:

Luke 7:7 – "But say the word and my servant will be healed".
Luke 8:50 – "Don't be afraid; just believe, and she will be healed".
Luke 9:2 – He sent them out to preach the kingdom of God and to heal the sick.
John 10:10 – "The thief comes only to steal and kill and destroy; I have come that they may have life, and have it to the full".
John 14:12-14 – "I tell you the truth, anyone who has faith in Me will do what I have been doing. He will do even greater things than these because I am going to the Father. And I will do whatever you ask in My name, so that the Son may bring glory to the Father. You may ask anything in My name, and I will do it".
2 Corinthians 4:16-18 -Therefore, we do not lose heart. Though outwardly we are wasting away, yet inwardly we are being renewed day by day. For our light and momentary troubles are achieving for us an eternal glory that far outweighs them all.
Hebrews 1:14 -Are not all angels ministering spirits sent to serve those who will inherit salvation?
James 5:14-16 - Is any one of you sick? He should call the elders of the church to pray over him and anoint him with oil in the name of the Lord. And the prayer offered in faith will make the sick person well; the Lord will raise him up. Therefore, confess your sins to each other and pray for each other so that you may be healed. The prayer of a righteous man is powerful and effective.
1 Peter 2:24 - He Himself bore our sins in His body on the tree, so that we might die to sins and live for righteousness; by His wounds you have been healed.
Revelation 21:4 – "He will wipe away every tear from their eyes. There will be no more death or mourning or crying or pain, for the old order of things has passed away."

Index: Caregiving Bible Verses

God's Words to pray for the <u>elderly</u>:

Psalm 73:26 - My flesh and my heart may fail, but God is the strength of my heart and my portion forever.

Psalm 92:12-15 - The righteous will flourish like a palm tree, they will grow like a cedar tree of Lebanon; planted in the house of the Lord, they will flourish in the courts of our God. They will still bear fruit in old age, they will stay fresh and green, proclaiming, "the Lord is upright; He is the Rock, and there is no wickedness in Him".

Proverbs 12:28 - In the way righteousness there is life; along that path is immortality.

Proverbs 16:31 - Gray hair is a crown of splendor; it is attained by a righteous life.

Isaiah 46:4 – Even to your old age and gray hairs, I am He, I am He who will sustain you.

Matthew 28:20 – "And surely I am with you always, to the very end of the age."

Philippians 3:20 & 21 – But our citizenship is in Heaven. And we eagerly await a Savior from there, the Lord Jesus Christ, who, by the power that enables Him to bring everything under His control, will transform our lowly bodies so that they will be like His glorious body.

1 Timothy 5:1 – Do not rebuke an older man harshly, but exhort him as if he were your father.

1 Timothy 5:3 & 5 – (3) Give proper recognition to those widows who are really in need. (5) The widow who really is in need and left all alone puts her hope in God and continues night and day to pray and to ask God for help.

Index: Caregiving Bible Verses

God's Words to pray for <u>peace</u>:

Psalm 4:8 – I will lie down and sleep in peace, for you alone, O Lord, make me dwell in safety.
Psalm 29:11 – The Lord gives strength to His people; the Lord blesses His people with peace.
Psalm 34:14 – Turn from evil and do good; seek peace and pursue it.
Psalm 144:3 – O Lord, what is man that You care for him, the son of man that You think of him?
Proverbs 12:20 – There is deceit in the hearts of those who plot evil, but joy for those who promote peace.
Proverbs 16:7 – When a man's ways are pleasing to the Lord, He makes even his enemies live in peace with him.
Isaiah 26:3 – You will keep in perfect peace him whose mind is steadfast, because he trusts in You.
Matthew 5:9 – Blessed are the peacemakers, for they will be called sons of God.
John 16:33 – "I have told you these things, so that in Me you may have peace".
Romans 15:13 – May the God of hope fill you with all joy and peace as you trust in Him, so that you may overflow with hope by the power of the Holy Spirit.
Philippians 4:6 & 7 – Do not be anxious about anything, but in everything, by prayer and petition, with thanksgiving, present your request to God. And the peace of God, which transcends all understanding, will guard your hearts and minds in Christ Jesus.
2 Thessalonians 3:16 – Now may the Lord of peace Himself give you peace at all times and in every way. The Lord be with all of you.

Index: Caregiving Bible Verses

God's Words to pray in <u>faith</u>:

Matthew 21:21 & 22 – Jesus replied, "I tell you the truth, if you have faith and do not doubt, not only can you do what was done to the fig tree, but also you can say to this mountain, go throw yourself into the sea, and it will be done. If you believe, you will receive whatever you ask for in prayer."

Mark 11:22 – "Have faith in God," Jesus answered.

Luke 1:37 – For nothing is impossible with God.

John 3:36 – Whoever believes in the Son has eternal life, but whoever rejects the Son will not see life, for God's wrath remains on him.

John 14:12 – "I tell you the truth, anyone who has faith in Me will do what I have been doing. He will do even greater things than these, because I am going to the Father."

Romans 10:17 – Consequently, faith comes from hearing the message, and the message is heard through the word of Christ.

1 Corinthians 2:4 & 5 – My message and my preaching were not with wise and persuasive words, but with a demonstration of the Spirit's power, so that your faith might not rest in men's wisdom, but on God's power.

2 Corinthians 5:7 – We live by faith, not by sight.

Philippians 1:6 – Being confident of this, that He who began a good work in you will carry it on to completion until the day of Christ Jesus.

Hebrews 11:1 – Now faith is being sure of what we hope for and certain of what we do not see.

Hebrews 11:8 – And without faith it is impossible to please God, because anyone who comes to Him must believe that He exists and that He rewards those who earnestly seek Him.

James 2:26 – As the body without the spirit is dead, so faith without deeds is dead.

Index: Caregiving Bible Verses

God's Words to pray about <u>loving others</u>:

Proverbs 10:12 – Hatred stirs up dissension, but love covers over all wrongs.

Matthew 22:37-39 – Jesus said, "Love the Lord your God with all your heart and with all your soul and with all your mind. This is the greatest commandment. And the second is like it: Love your neighbor as yourself."

Mark 8:2 – "I have compassion for these people; they have already been with me three days and have nothing to eat."

John 13:34 – "A new command I give you; Love one another. As I have loved you, so you must love one another. By this all men will know that you are my disciples, if you love one another."

John 14:15 – "If you love me, you will obey what I command."

John 15:13 – "Greater love has no one than this, that he lay down his life for his friends."

1 Corinthians 13:4-8 – Love is patience, love is kind. It does not envy, it does not boast, it is not proud. It is not rude, it is not self-seeking, it is not easily angered, it keeps no records of wrong. Love does not delight in evil but rejoices with the truth. It always protects, always trusts, always hopes, always perseveres. Love never fails.

1 Corinthians 13:13 – And now these three remain: faith, hope and love. But the greatest of these is love.

1 Corinthians 14:1 – Follow the way of love and eagerly desire spiritual gifts, especially the gift of prophesy.

Galatians 5:22 – But the fruit of the Spirit is love, joy, peace, patience, kindness, goodness, faithfulness, gentleness, and self-control.

2 Timothy 1:7 – For God did not give us a spirit of timidity, but a spirit of power, of love, and of self-discipline.

Index: Caregiving Bible Verses

God's Words to pray about <u>loving others</u>:

1 Peter 1:8-9 – Though you have not seen Him, you love Him; and even though you do not see Him now, you believe in Him and are filled with an inexpressible and glorious joy, for you are receiving the goal of your faith, the salvation of your souls.

1 John 3:16 – This is how we know what love is: Jesus Christ laid down His life for us, and we ought to lay down our lives for our brothers.

1 John 3:18 – Dear children, let us not love with words or tongue but with actions and in truth.

1 John 4:7-12 – Dear friends, let us love one another, for love comes from God. Everyone who loves has been born of God and knows God. Whoever does not love does not know God., because God is love. This is how God showed his love among us: He sent His one and only Son into the world that we might live through Him. This is love: not that we loved God, but that He loved us and sent his Son as an atoning sacrifice for our sins. Dear friends, since God so loved us, we ought also to love one another. No one has ever seen God; but if we love one another, God lives in us and His love is made complete in us.

1 John 4:16 – And so we know and rely on the love God has for us. God is love. Whoever lives in love, loves in God, and God in him.

1 John 4:18 – There is no fear in love. But perfect love drives out fear, because fear has to do with punishment. The one who fears is not made perfect in love.

1 John 4:19-21 – We love because He first loved us. If anyone says, "I love God," yet hates his brother, he is a liar. For anyone who does not love his brother, whom he has seen, cannot love God, whom he has not seen. And He has given this command: Whoever loves God must also love his brother.

Index: Caregiving Bible Verses

God's Words to pray for <u>Salvation</u>:

Matthew 6:33 – But seek first His Kingdom and His righteousness and all these things will be given to you as well.

Matthew 28:18-19 – Then Jesus came to them and said, "All authority in Heaven and on earth has been given Me. Therefore, go and make disciples of all nations, baptizing them in the name of the Father and of the Son and of the Holy Spirit."

Mark 2:17 – On hearing this, Jesus said to them, "It is not the healthy who need a doctor, but the sick. I have not come to call the righteous, but sinners."

Mark 16:15 – He said to them, "Go into all the world and preach the good news to all creation."

John 3:3 – In reply Jesus declared, "I tell you the truth, no one can see the kingdom of God unless he is born-again."

John 3:16 – "For God so loved the world that He gave His one and only Son, that whoever believes in Him shall not perish, but have eternal life."

John 5:24 – "I tell you the truth, whoever hears My Word and believes Him who sent Me has eternal life and will not be condemned; he has crossed over from death to life."

John 11:25-26 – Jesus said to her, "I am the resurrection and the life. He who believes in Me will live, even though he dies; and whoever lives and believes in Me will never die."

John 14:6 – Jesus answered, "I am the Way and the Truth and the Life. No one comes to the Father except through me."

Acts 4:12 – Salvation is found in no one else, for there is no other name under heaven given to men by which we must be saved.

Romans 6:23 – For the wages of sin is death, but the gift of God is eternal life in Christ Jesus our Lord.

Index: Caregiving Bible Verses

God's Words to pray for <u>Salvation</u>:

Romans 5:8 – But God demonstrated His own love for us in this: While we were still sinners, Christ died for us.

Romans 10:9 – That if you confess with your mouth, "Jesus is Lord", and believe in your heart that God raised Him from the dead, you will be saved.

Galatians 3:26-27 – You are all sons of God through faith in Christ Jesus, for all of you who were baptized into Christ have clothed yourselves with Christ.

Ephesians 2:4-5 – But because of His great love for us, God, who is rich in mercy, made us alive with Christ even when we were dead in transgressions – it is by grace you have been saved.

Ephesians 2:8 & 9 – For it is by grace you have been saved, through faith – and this is not from yourselves, it is the gift of God – not by works, so that no one can boast.

Titus 3:4-5 – But when the kindness and love of God our Savior appeared, He saved us, not because of righteous things we had done, but because of His mercy.

1 Peter 2:24 – He Himself bore our sins in His body on the tree, so that we might die to sins and live for righteousness; by His wounds you have been healed.

1 John 1:9 – If we confess our sins, He is faithful and just and will forgive us our sins and purify us from all unrighteousness.

1 John 2:2 He is the atoning sacrifice for our sins, and not only for ours but also for the sins of the whole world.

1 John 3:4 – But you know that He appeared so that He might take away our sins.

Index: Caregiving Bible Verses

God's Word about the <u>Holy Spirit</u>:

Joel 2:28-32 – "I will pour out My Sprit on all people, your sons and daughters will prophesy, your old men will dream dreams, your young men will see visions. Even on My servants, both men and women, I will pour out My Spirit in those days.

Matthew 3:11 – I baptize you with water for repentance. But after me will come one who is more powerful than I, whose sandals I am not fit to carry. He will baptize you with the Holy Spirit and with fire.

Luke 11:13 – "If you then, though you are evil, know how to give good gifts to your children, how much more will your Father in Heaven give the Holy Spirit to those who ask Him!"

Luke 24:49 – I am going to send you what My Father has promised; but stay in the city until you have been clothed with power from on high."

John 14:15-17 – "If you love Me, you will obey what I command. And I will ask the Father, and He will give you another Counselor to be with you forever – the Spirit of Truth."

John 14:26 – But the Counselor, the Holy Spirit, whom the Father will send in My name, will teach you all things and will remind you of everything I have said to you.

John 20:22 – And with that, He breathed on them and said, "Receive the Holy Spirit."

Acts 1:8 – "But you will receive power when the Holy Spirit comes on you; and you will be My witnesses in Jerusalem, and in all Judea and Samaria, and to the ends of the earth."

Acts 2:4 – All of them were filled with the Holy Spirit and began to speak in other tongues as the Spirit enabled them.

Romans 8:9 – You, however are controlled not by the sinful nature, but by the Holy Spirit, if the Spirit of God lives in you.

Index: Caregiving Bible Verses

God's Word about the Holy Spirit:

Romans 8:26 – In the same way, the Spirit helps us in our weakness. We do not know what we ought to pray for, but the Spirit Himself intercedes for us with groans that words cannot express.
1 Corinthians 12:1 – Now about Spiritual gifts, brothers, I do not want you to be ignorant.
1 Corinthians 12:4 – There are different kinds of gifts, but the same Spirit.
1 Corinthians 12:7-11 – Now to each one the manifestation of the Spirit is given for the common good. To one there is given through the Spirit, the message of wisdom, to another the message of knowledge by means of the Spirit, to another faith by the same Spirit, to another the gifts of healing, by that one Spirit, to another miraculous Powers, to another prophecy, to another distinguishing between spirits, to another speaking in different kinds of tongues, and to still another the interpretation of tongues. All these are the work of one and the same Spirit, and He gives them to each one, just as He determines.
1 Corinthians 14:1 – Follow the way of love and eagerly desire the Spiritual gifts, especially the gift of prophecy.
Ephesians 4:4 & 5 – There is one body and one Spirit – just as you were called to one hope when you were called – one Lord, one faith, one baptism; one God and Father of all, who is over all and through all and in all.
Colossians 2:4 & 5 – I tell you this so that no one may deceive you by fine-sounding arguments. For though I am absent from you in the body, I am present with you in Spirit and delight to see how orderly you are and how firm your faith in Christ is.
Jude 1:20 – But you, dear friends, build yourselves up in your most holy faith and pray in the Holy Spirit.

Index: Caregiving Bible Verses

God's Word to pray for <u>caregivers</u>:

Numbers 6:24-26 – The Lord bless you and keep you; the Lord make His face shine upon you and be gracious to you; the lord turn His face toward you and give you peace.

Proverbs 3:5 & 6 – Trust in the Lord with all your heart and lean not on your only understanding; in all your ways acknowledge Him, and He will make your path straight.

Proverbs 15:7 – When a man's ways are pleasing to the Lord, He makes even his enemies live in peace with him.

Isaiah 55:6 – Seek the Lord while He may be found; call on Him while He is near.

Matthew 25:21 – "Well done, good and faithful servant! You have been faithful with a few things; I will put you in charge of many things."

Matthew 25:37-40 – "Then the righteous will answer Him, Lord, when did we see You hungry and feed You, or thirsty and give You something to drink? When did we see You a stranger and invite You in, or needing clothes and clothe You? When did we see You sick or in prison and go to visit You? The king will reply, I tell you the truth, whatever you did for one of the least of these brothers of mine, you did for Me."

John 14:27 – Peace I leave with you, My peace I give you. I do not give to you as the world gives. Do not let your hearts be troubled and do not be afraid.

Romans 8:28 – And we know that in all things God works for the good of those who love Him, who have been called according to His purpose.

Romans 8:29 – For those God foreknew He also predestined to be conformed to the likeness of His Son, that He might be the firstborn among many brothers. And those He predestined, He also called, those He called, He also justified, He also glorified.

Index: Caregiving Bible Verses

God's Word to pray for <u>caregivers:</u>

Romans 8:31 – What shall we say in response to this? If God is for us, who can be against us?

Romans 8:34 – Christ Jesus, who died – more than that, who was raised to life – is at the right hand of God and is also interceding for us.

Romans 8:35 – Who shall separate us from the love of Christ? Shall trouble or hardship or persecution or famine or nakedness or danger or sword?

Romans 8:37 – No, in all things we are more than conquerors through Him who loved us.

Romans 8:38 – For I am convinced that neither death nor life, neither angels nor demons, neither the present nor the future, nor any powers, neither height nor depth, nor anything else in all creation, will be able to separate us from the love of God that is in Christ Jesus our Lord.

Romans 12:7 – If a man's gift is serving, let him serve; if it is teaching, let him teach; if it is encouraging, let him encourage; if it is contributing to the needs of others, let him give generously; if it is leadership, let him govern diligently; if it is showing mercy, let him do it cheerfully.

Romans 12:13 – Share with God's people who are in need. Practice hospitality.

Romans 15:17 – Therefore, I glory in Christ Jesus in my service to God.

1 Corinthians 10:24 – Nobody should seek his own good, but the good of others.

Ephesians 5:1 – Be imitators of God, therefore, as dearly loved children and live a life of love, just as Christ loved us and gave Himself up for us as a fragrant offering and sacrifice to God.

2 Timothy 2:24 – And the Lord's servant must not quarrel; instead, he must be kind to everyone, able to teach, not resentful.

1 Peter 5:7 – Cast all your anxiety on Him because He cares for you.

Added Material / Dementia Help

25 creative pastimes that can encourage people with dementia.

Activities should be: simple, repetitive, one or two steps, focusing on abilities not on limitations, age-appropriate, related to past roles, be normalization in nature, and stress free. Most here are included for the individual with moderate to severe dementia.

Avoid activities that require: new learning, sequencing, abstract concepts, large group interactions, complex supplies, noise, glare, confusion, rushing, etc.

Objectives for the activities offered: a purposeful use of time, produce positive behavior, reduce negative behavior, anxiousness, stress, or combativeness.

Normalization and Physical Activities:
1. Washing dishes, cups, spoons, and forks in a basin of soapy water
2. Stacking things such as cups, small books, organizing pictures, etc.
3. Stuffing envelopes with cards
4. Folding clothes or towels, putting into laundry basket
5. Give person a wet cloth, ask them to help you clean the table.
6. Fill penny holders (suggested only for those who are not known for putting foreign objects into their mouths)
7. Allow them to do safe jobs when baking or cooking, such as stirring, pouring, peeling, measuring, rolling out dough, shucking peas, tasting.
8. Provide a large box of greeting cards, they will enjoy looking through them. Help them send a card or use cards in craft projects.
9. Read a cookbook together, then ask them to help you to make out a shopping list for ingredients needed to make a recipe.

Added Material / Dementia Help (cont.)

10. Normalization activities should include outings: Sensory Strolls, Museums, Grocery stores, Dollar Stores, Park settings, Zoo, inviting a friend to visit, etc.
11. Flower / vegetable planting in pots, flower arranging, watering the garden
12. Pet visits
13. Table setting and napkin folding
14. Lead an exercise routine, balloon volleyball, ball throw, etc.
15. Playing hand bells or small drums, singing, clapping
16. Coupon clipping

Cognitive-based activities:
17. Create a picture book with them by choosing and cutting out all magazine pictures of a certain subject-animals, babies, flowers, food, etc. (you can laminate them to put in an album. Use it for encouraging a verbal response, discussion, reminiscing, or as an identification exercise).
18. Organizing/sorting tools, socks, playing cards, etc. according to size, shape, color, or purpose.
19. Reading: for those who still have this skill, encourage them to read newspaper articles, comic strip, joke book, greeting cards, poems.
20. Writing: Help them write out a message on greeting cards, etc.
21. Find the Right Page Activity: Using a magazine or a newspaper, ask person to find following sections or photos having to do with children, sports, business, food, animals, clothing, etc.
22. Reminisce with them looking through a family album.
23. Tracing activity with age-appropriate templates
24. Card games, Bingo, Board games (adapted to person's ability).
25. Create fill in the blank sheet with simple questions or ask open-ended questions.

www.ingramcontent.com/pod-product-compliance
Lightning Source LLC
Chambersburg PA
CBHW061721020426
42331CB00006B/1027

* 9 7 8 0 6 9 2 9 2 1 6 0 9 *